THE AGE OF THE HEART:
THE BIRTH OF A NEW HEAVEN AND A NEW EARTH
A MESSAGE FROM THE CHRIST IN YOU

TAKE HEART PUBLICATIONS
13315 Buttermilk Bend
North San Juan, CA 95960
www.takeheartpublications.com
ISBN 978-1-58469-703-9

Cover and editorial design by Alejandro Arrojo
Computer production by
Patty Arnold, *Menagerie Design and Publishing*
Manufactured in the United States of America

The Age
of the
Heart

*The Birth of a New Heaven
and a New Earth*

Table of contents

How This Work Originated

On October 3, 2021, a week after having completed the reception and transcription of a trilogy of works to be published under the title Truly Beloved, while in silent prayer a choir of countless angels from Heaven presented themselves to me. From their hearts emerged a hymn of praise and gratitude to the Love of Loves for having called us into existence.

Before their arrival, my soul was submerged in a deep peace, a stillness that surrounds everything in holiness, happiness, and purity, a state of indescribable joy. The senses of the body were silenced, and a kind of serene and harmonious "whistling" was received by my physical ears and felt throughout my body. A sensation of being caressed by a soft, dancing breeze covered my entire face.

All this and other things full of beauty and purity happen suddenly as a prelude to the coming of such manifestations so that my humanity prepares to receive what Heaven is about to reveal. My soul knows, in a way that cannot be put into words, that the song of ineffable beauty that the angels sing and express from their hearts, is constantly being sung in creation. It is a response to the Divine Mother for having been called into existence, for having been given life. It is an eternal hosanna that filiation sings to the Creator of all that is beautiful, holy, and perfect; to the one who is beyond all names, words and symbols. Within that heavenly song of indescribable beauty is the voice of Christ—that is, pure thought.

In each visit, images, music, and symbolic visions show me what constitutes the message of the moment, which is later transcribed into written words. Once the images and symbols are given, Jesus of Nazareth, the incarnated Christ, comes in all his glory, humanity, and divinity. It is he who dictated the words that make up the chapters of this work, and instructed me in the knowledge of them. By the word "dictation," I must explain the following.

Without any volition on my part except for my willingness, I begin to listen with the ears of my spirit to the song that always precedes these visions or revelations. It is a wordless song that I experience as the music of the soul, a song long forgotten, but now remembered. Listening to those heavenly notes, my humanity is submerged in incomparable joy and wrapped in a peace without compare. My soul and my body are embraced in the love of Christ. Everything is joy, perpetual serenity, purity, and ineffable beatitude. My being remains captivated in ecstasy which I wish will never leave.

Simultaneously, what the will of God provides is shown to me in my consciousness like a clear, sharp movie or vision. It is given to me to see the creative processes of God, how time was born in unity with space, and how matter would remain contained within time and space and subject to them. I have seen how the three dimensions of material reality, time-space-matter, are an expression of the mind that has limited itself. All three are within the separated mind and not the other way around. They are an extension of it.

I have also been shown how universal consciousness is walking towards the heart of God. These things were revealed to me and constitute the content of this work. There are others matters that, although made known to me, are not part of these writings due to the disposition of the voice that speaks in favor of the truth and lives eternally in my being.

Each one of the visions or "movies" that I was given to see became a chapter of this work. After seeing what the Spirit of wisdom wants me to remember and see, then the voice of Christ, in the most holy presence of Jesus, who is also sometimes present with Mary, explains to me the meaning of the vision. Then he dictates to me the meaning that should be written.

This "dictation" is accomplished without words. It is an infused knowledge transmitted from the mind of Christ to mine, and from the heart of love to the center of my spirit. In that flow of wisdom, from the source of beautiful knowledge to my being, everything that needs to be known is perfectly known. The words that give expression to this work emerge by themselves; I put no thought into them. The thinking mind does not create the words, the syntaxes, or the idiomatic structures. The words simply flow because of the union between the source of beautiful knowledge and the living expression of my humanity, which becomes a pen in the hand of love.

At other times, dictations are given to me in the form of Pure thought, that is, without any visible presence, although audible and sensitive—Christ in his pure incorporeal essence.

There is a message in the fact that dictations are carried out in the presence of both Jesus and Mary, as well as in the pure abstraction of the voice of Christ. The method of the message itself shows how we are in the time of union—the union of the feminine and the masculine, of the divine and the human, of the corporal and the spiritual. In short, it is a demonstration within time of the return to the unity of being, that is, of the transcendence of dualistic polarities.

All this is a prelude to the time of the fullness of love, in which Heaven and Earth will recognize and see each other as one, just as they always have been and forever will be.

What is meant by all this is that from these times the Voice of God will continue to speak to humanity as much as is necessary, but will no longer do so in separate forms but through symbols of unity, until the symbols cease to be necessary and His sweet voice is heard without interruption in the wordless language of love, the language of pure souls, the language of being.

In the visions I was shown the story of creation, the evolution of consciousness, and the fate of all things. The origin of time, the path of souls, and the history of humanity were also revealed to me as part of the expression of universal consciousness.

I have been given to understand that the knowledge that was revealed to me in this manifestation exists in everyone, since it is part of our shared reality. For this reason, I believe that the most accurate word to describe these messages would not be "revelations" but "remembrances." This work is an expression of universal mind, which testifies to the fact that we are remembering, individually and collectively, where we came from, where we are, and where we are going. In other words, remembering the truth that we have come to remember—the truth of who we are.

With love in Christ,

Sebastián Blaksley
Buenos Aires, Argentina

Editor's Note: God has no gender but languages do. The reader will note that the Deity is referred to in this work sometimes as masculine, sometimes as feminine, and sometimes as "Mother-Father God." The intent is to reflect the universality of the Divine while staying within the conventions of the English language to which most readers are accustomed.

A Note from Sebastián Concerning the Timing of the Age of the Heart

After receiving the messages presented in this work, it was pointed out to me that it is often said herein that the Age of the Heart has already begun, but nowhere is it clearly stated when that significant shift took place. Therefore I asked that question, and Angel responded to me in the presence of Jesus and Mary and a choir of uncountable angels. I was given the gift of experiencing the beauty and smile of the nameless Angel, a smile full of love and appreciation for our interest in knowing more about how the new is being manifested.

Angel told me that the Age of the Heart began not in one particular hour or day but in one "interval of time" consisting of a period of seven years beginning December, 2007, through December, 2014, with a significant quantum leap in 2012. During that window of time the portal of the New was open and the "Flow of the Energy of Truth," as Angel called it, started to flow from the Heart of Christ to the whole universe. Angel said that this energy of truth is flooding all of creation with a magnitude never before seen in history and that it "cannot be stopped."

Additionally, Angel said that a new quantum leap is occurring from 2021 to 2033. After that period, we will see the New Light more vividly than ever. In particular, an event of "universal consciousness" will take place in 2033, a significant moment for all humanity, a Universal event that "all will see"—including everyone and everything, regardless of the state of consciousness they have achieved at that moment. Even if someone denies the Truth, they will see it anyway. Even babies ready to be born will witness it. Everyone will see it externally; some will see it both externally and internally.

Further, this universal event includes all planes of existence, so not only all human beings on Earth at that moment will know of it, but also every single soul (mind) in all dimensions.

Angel said that ancient predictions, including the Mayans and many others, were based on truth that brothers and sisters in those cultures received from Heaven, and that all of them came from the Voice of Christ. For example, Angel told me that when Maya culture spoke of the end of the world being in 2012, the original expression was that 2012 would be both the end (death) of the old humanity and the birth of the New. In my own tradition, I note that Pope Francis was elected on March 13th, 2013, reflecting a big transformation for the Catholic Church, part of a transmutation for all religious institutions.

Finally, Angel said: "Those who were and are consciously connected to Christ's Life (that is, connected to Christ mind or consciousness in an uncountable variety of ways) made this possible. The New would never manifest without those brothers and sisters who, in so many different ways, dedicate their hearts to Christ."

CHRIST, a definition

Although the word "Christ" as used in this work is sometimes linked to a masculine pronoun, "Christ" is a much broader term that is not limited to any person or even any creature. Upon asking for a definition, Sebastián received the following on March 25, 2023:

Christ is the identity that all creation shares in God. It is what makes a tree a tree, a fish a fish, and a human a human. This Christ identity is what makes each being unique, eternal, immutable, and holy since it is the essence of each created being, both having its own identity and also always united to source. Christ is the true nature of each being.

Introduction

Beloved of my heart, soul full of holiness! In our love is truth revealed; in our union, wisdom. Together we create new life.

I have come to take your hand, your humanity, and your time to bring light to minds and peace to hearts through these words. The world needs to know. That is why I come to reveal the path of creation and to answer the question that exists in the hearts of our brothers and sisters which goes like this: "Where am I and where am I going?"

Observe, my beloved, that the part of the question that asks, "Where do I come from?" has been omitted because it has already been answered in the writings previously given to you to share with the world. If you stop and meditate serenely on what is said here, you will discover a direct relationship between all these words. They are part of a whole. Knowing the origin of your existence is also knowing your reality and destiny, since they are one and the same. However, because the mind and the heart sometimes need to separate symbols and then give meaning to the whole in human language, successive writings have been created of which these are an integral part.

These words are directed to the Christ consciousness in you. We are no longer talking about a mind or a heart, because you have reached the state of fullness of being in which you recognize that they are inseparable in your holy humanity. So there is no reason to distinguish between one and the other. We call the unity of mind and heart "consciousness of being." It is to your consciousness of being that this expression of love and truth is directed.

My voice represented in this work will go where it needs to go. The soul that receives it will understand why they are the daughter or son of the light that shines everywhere. I do not speak to anyone in particular, because that there is no such thing as an individual being has already been gleefully recognized and accepted. We are speaking from the totality of Source to the unity of creation.

Universal consciousness is the perfect extension of divine consciousness, as one embraces the other. We use two terms to be more easily understood. In this revelation, the consciousness of the Creator manifests itself to the consciousness of the created in the unity of love and wisdom. The two form a relationship: Created and Creator. Origin and destination. Alpha and Omega.

Said simply, these writings are a manifestation of the knowledge of Christ, revealing himself out of love for humanity—a love that will be present for all eternity. They are directed to the center of your being, and because of the unity of being, to the center of universal consciousness. Remember that we are one mind, one heart, one soul. United we are the light of life.

Pure soul! As you go through this work, it is likely that you will come across revelations that the thinking mind does not understand and are therefore difficult to accept. That simply comes from the habit of using what is learned as a source of knowledge, rather than allowing the truth to be revealed. Do not let this stop you. Let us continue together, hand in hand, until all that has to be said is said by reason of our perfect wisdom. You will see how the whole carries within itself a gift that the part alone does not yield.

Absorb each word given to you here as if they are dew drops from the sky. Let yourself be carried away by them. Feel them. Embrace them with all your soul and all your being. Allow the power that resides in them to embed itself in your humanity and to extend beyond you because of our love. This is how we transmit them to the whole world and all of creation—not by virtue of the old laws but of the spirit of Mother-Father God who makes all things new.

Remember, beloved of my divine heart, nothing is impossible for me. Therefore, neither is it for you because you are one with me. My voice reaches the center of who you are. Your soul knows who is speaking. It knows the voice of truth. It recognizes the wisdom of God, because it exists and moves within it. Do not deny your being the sweetness of my voice nor the joy of remaining united in the sanctity of being! United we are the House of Truth, the Heaven of Peace in which our brothers and sisters long to dwell, the purest extension of the wisdom of Heaven. Together we create the new Heaven and the new Earth. These words bear witness.

Blessed are you who listen to my voice and follow me.

Jesus, the Christ in you

1.

Journey of
The Soul

I. The Origin of Everything

Every soul makes a journey without distance from the heart of God to the knowledge of Christ. Although both are a unit and reside in divine essence, this "journey" is necessary for the individuation of being to take place. As a soul, you have been moving from one point to another. A "point" or "movement" should not be understood literally, since reality is infinitely one, without parts, spaces, or places to go. Nevertheless, a movement toward the realization of consciousness of being does occur.

The created being emerges from the Source of life and is impelled to know itself as what it is—an expression of perfect love. This knowledge can only be achieved in truth—in its essence, reality, and abode. Only when this is reached can it be said that fullness has been reached, since knowledge and the created are one and the same. From Mother-Father God proceeds being, created out of pure holy love, directed towards Christ.

What happens in the soul also happens in universal consciousness with which it is inextricably joined, and vice versa. The path that each soul travels is the same as that which humanity as a whole travels. You sprout from my divine heart.

The gift of freedom to deliberately choose love is revealed to you. You walk the path that leads you to the knowledge of who you really are—to make the option for love. And then you merge into the Sacred Heart, the unity of my divine being and true creation. Simply put, you come from love, in love you know yourself, and to love you return in the perfect knowledge of your eternal uniqueness.

The same occurs with what we will call collective consciousness. Every soul belongs to a collective. Thus we can speak of the "human family." The infinite sum of all the collectives, or groups of creations, makes up the filiation.

When you decided to know yourself outside the source of beautiful knowledge of the truth, you joined a type of knowledge that was not actually knowledge. This decision was not irrevocable because it was actually a choice not to meet yourself. You chose based on the notion that it was unnecessary to join the knowledge of the truth about who you are. This decision cost you the consciousness of the heaven of your being. For this to be possible, there had to exist, in advance, a collective consciousness that you could join based on the denial of knowledge, and therefore of being. However, that option was destined not to last, since it carried within itself the foundations of dissolution.

The denial of being necessarily implies the cessation of existence. Since that is impossible—since eternity is your source and reality—by making that choice you create a state of conflict, a kingdom of chaos where you cannot dwell in peace. But in it there is an exit, which is nothing other than the same door through which you entered: your self-determination. How you get to the point where you will exercise your free will to make the fundamental choice to live in the truth is what the experience you call "the world" is all about—the world being a dimension of time, matter, and space apparently separate from God.

Naturally, a reality disjointed from its Source of love is impossible. In response, the mind made inaccurate use of its faculties. Instead of co-creating in Christ, it fabricated fantasies. This capacity of the soul has nothing to do with original creation.

II. Love: The Only Reality

God has no fantasies about anything; neither does your being. From a system of thought based on the imagination, only a world of images can emerge. And so it happened—not in divine creation, but in your particular experience, within the collective that was in harmony with that experience.

You will always belong to universal consciousness, regardless of how you conceive of it. You can remain united to the consciousness of Light or to a collective unconsciousness. In both cases you will belong to a "group" to which you adhere. Nothing in creation exists without being attached to something greater than itself. The part cannot do without the whole; to be a part, it must be part of something. That something is the totality to which it adheres. Thus identity is always a shared issue. No creature can be the source of its own identity. Only Christ is the source of true identity, because only Mother-Father God is the Source of meaning.

You may wonder why we speak of the past in a work that reveals the new. We do so that you can understand more clearly where you are. You have reached the point where—as an individuated soul and humanity—you have returned to the knowledge of who you really are. That is, you have reached the state of the unity of being. You are no longer a being without reason; you are no longer denying the truth. You are love, reintegrated.

Therefore, everything is new, not because of what the intellect can understand or imagine, but because the consciousness of the truth that you are is co-creating in unity with universal consciousness. A conscious connection between your humanity and God has been reestablished.

This is the first time that has happened on your soul's journey. I shall explain.

On the plane of humanity, you were never separate from the Source of beautiful love, for if that had occurred, you would cease to exist. However, when you were created you were endowed with free will as an aspect of who you are. Freedom is Mother-Father God's will for Her creations. Otherwise, God Herself could not be free. When emerging from the Divine Heart, the soul carries within itself the seed of a question, a question which exists in every living being, not just in the human soul.

This fundamental "question" did not exist as a question, properly speaking, in the primal state. The mind had not yet conceived the language of separation, which uses words that can never be understood by everyone or everything, for that is its purpose. The fundamental question is actually an appeal: a call from God to Her creature. It is the Voice of Love calling the soul to choose love. All creation carries within itself that call.

Since the mental state that arose in the soul upon separation interprets everything based on the language of words upon which the mind elaborates, the call became a question. Nevertheless, it is still an appeal, a loving invitation that lives in all hearts. It is the question that you carried within your soul which would not leave you alone, and had you ask, "What am I?" Behind it is the call to choose love as your only reality and, with it, the truth of what you are. Ultimately, it is the voice of Christ that over and over asks, "Will you give me your soul?" This request that love makes of love is universal, and also contains within itself the grace of your essential free will.

Love and freedom cannot be separate. They are the same. Thus, every being in creation wants to be free. Captivity will never be to your liking, for freedom is your natural state of being. If you lacked free will, you could neither love nor live in love, which would make you stop being. Since love created you as an extension of itself, you are called to exercise your freedom in love.

III. Freedom and Will

All of humanity has come to the world of space, time, and form to exercise free will in union with truth. That's what the journey of the soul is all about—a path from the non-exercise of freedom towards the fullness of being. None can reach full realization without consciously exercising their freedom. God knows this perfectly. She is as free as you. All Her creations are.

I am also reminding you, beloved of my divinity, that none are obliged to love. You can easily verify this. You cannot force someone to love you, and no one can force you to love something or someone, nor to stop loving. Love cannot be imposed. Neither can it be learned. That is what makes beliefs and systems of thought powerless in the face of reality. Nothing can be imposed on love. In this resides its sovereignty, its strength, and its unshakable peace.

Time has been given for you to exercise your free will—that is, to answer the fundamental question that the Creator has imprinted on all hearts, calling you to accept perfect love as your only reality and your being. And in this way, to enjoy the wonders that love created and eternally creates in union with truth. Likewise, space, the physical body, the personality, and everything that exists in the material universe has been granted you to exercise this fundamental option. Everything is available to contribute to your perfect fulfillment, which you achieve by living in freedom as a child of God.

The only difference that exists between people is simply between those who have already chosen, and those who still postpone choosing, a difference which will always be respected by God. This discernment is essential to this revelation. We no longer see some as good or bad, wise or ignorant, right or wrong. We look only from the perspective of truth. The difference lies only in the fact of exercising free will or not. All will do so in due time. Those who have already responded to the call from On High continue their existence on the eternal path of holy love, hand-in-hand with Christ whom they have freely accepted as truth—their only reality and the Source of their being.

You may wonder: why do those who have consciously chosen love and yearn with all their hearts to live in divine unity, continue to be in the world for a while? Listen, my beloved. What other reason could there be but to extend love? They are love, souls who have reached the unity of being on Earth. They know that there are sisters and brothers still asleep in the dream of oblivion, a state of non-choice, arising from the existence of an internal conflict that leads the mind to not decide.

They know this because they have experienced it. Their memories have been healed by love, so that they will not leave the world by their free choice until they have completed their part in the work of the universal awakening to love. That work, like everything else in creation, is a collaborative endeavor. They will not leave the world until they give what they are called to give, so that the Earthly world awakens to truth. Being consciously united to Christ, they do so in perfect harmony with the will of God, with which they are eternally united. They extend the divine light of their being despite what may come to pass on the byways of the world because they know the truth. They are frightened of nothing. They know that there is no such thing as Heaven over there and Earth over here. They know unity. They enjoy spreading the love that they are, now and forever.

Souls who have exercised their true freedom remain united with love wherever they go, rest in peace in love's arms wherever they are, and experience what they experience. Their lives no longer belong to them, for they have given them to Christ, the source of all truth and holiness. Thus, the only thing that can be done is realized in them and through them: the eternal extension of God. Knowing that they are eternally loved with a love that has no beginning or end and in whose reality the fullness of being is found, they eternally enjoy perfect fulfillment.

2.

The Movement of Consciousness

I. The Whole and the Part

J ust as the soul makes a journey without distance from having been created in the pure potentiality of being towards the awareness of its identity—towards the full knowledge of what it is—universal consciousness takes the same journey. Both the particular soul and the collective consciousness with which it is joined are part of the same rhythmic movement. They are united.

It is not possible to understand the path of the soul without knowing that of the universal consciousness to which it belongs, and vice versa. Both are part of a totality that cannot be separated if one wishes to understand things in the light of truth. To answer the question of what humanity is, where it is, or where it is going, you only need to know what is happening in your own reality, for there is no difference between the journey of creation and your own. The created always perform the same journey, a path to self-knowledge. This knowledge means not only knowing, but pure acceptance. This is why fully accepting what is brings the peace of consciousness.

Acceptance and awareness go hand-in-hand because not accepting what is as it is means that you believe that it may be something other than what it really is—and not in fantasy. How could you wish for things to be different from what they are if you were not harboring the belief of the possibility of such a thing? To put it another way, not accepting the reality of things as they are is a sign that you believe that there may be another source of knowledge, different from reality. Is this not a denial of reality itself? For what other reason would one deny it, but to replace it with something else?

Well-loved soul, reality is the only source of beautiful knowledge because it is the eternal extension of Mother-Father God, the Source and purpose of knowledge. It can only be accessed when the mind and heart, united in truth, are at peace. Serenity of spirit is necessary to allow the benevolence of truth to be present because love only makes an appearance where peace abides. And since truth is the voice and power of love, only when it enters the human mind and heart can humanity receive revelation.

Those first brothers and sisters who once walked the Earth, although human, had not reached the degree of consciousness that would allow them to conceive the idea of God or of love.

Humanity did not always express its longing for union with the transcendent or its drive to search for truth. Consciousness dictates the creature's expression. The first children of God who stepped upon the Earth carried within them a blessed seed which is now a beautiful flower displayed in your humanity. In the same way, you carry within your heart a divine seed which will manifest as a new flower of holiness that will embellish creation. This is how the universe moves towards the full consciousness of love.

To understand more clearly what is being remembered in this dialogue, it is important that you see what is created as an expression of consciousness, not the other way around. While both are a unit, at least for now it will be easier for you to see one as a manifestation of the other. With this idea in mind, you can see how human life is an expression of the kind of universal consciousness to which it is attached in the present. In turn, this is, to a certain degree, in union with truth. In reality the Earthly path that you and your sisters and brothers in Christ travel is but a path back to the Mother/Father God's house.

II. The Consciousness of Being

When we speak of humanity, we mean the present expression of your nature in time and space, not to be confused with the eternal manifestation of your being. What you are does not cease to be what it is when you have fulfilled your purpose on the plane of material expression. In heavenly humanity, that is, the life of what you are in full divine realization, you remain united to all realities manifested and yet to be manifested, which are always in harmony with the being of pure love that gives them existence. In other words, you live fully conscious in divine reality.

Consciousness, which is what you really are, manifests itself to know itself. Your physical humanity—your Earthly experience—is a means of knowing yourself and thus a way to respond to the call of love. This is undoubtedly an indirect means, since knowledge finds its source in God. Nevertheless, this is the chosen means for your full realization of what you are, a perfect means since its end is perfection. There is nothing in your humanity that should not be embraced by love, because all of it allows you to get to where you truly want to be—to live the life of God consciously in the unity of being.

The knowledge revealed here in human words was not available before this time. It existed as pure potentiality in the soul, but had not manifested. The unmanifested is unknown. Just as humanity was not always aware of the existence of the Supreme Being, neither was it always aware of the truth that that Being was love and nothing but love. Once humanity reached the degree of consciousness capable of making this truth a reality, it was able to take the next step. That step is now taking place in the present creation story: full acceptance that not only is the Creator love, but also the created, being an eternally holy unity.

You may think all this is not of great relevance. But it is. It represents a quantum leap in universal consciousness. It is as transformative as the expansion of consciousness that led the world to create religions, spirituality and philosophy, from which came the world you experience. Every single system of government, human organization, or development in the sciences is the effect of the universal consciousness that gives rise to it. This is why in the past it was impossible for the expressions in the world today to exist. Everything, even consciousness, has its time within the realm of time.

It is one thing to have a worldview in which you conceive of yourself as a body, adrift in a fearful and dangerous world, and an altogether different one to know yourself as the well-loved daughter or son of a Mother-Father God of infinite love and limitless power whose only will is that you be eternally happy. For this, God has made you heir to His honor and glory. From one view emerges a world of struggle, competition, and survival, a world without mercy; from the other, a world in which God is praised in the eternal reality of love, not as a belief, but as a living expression of what is dictated by the heart united in holiness with the mind.

III. The Light of Truth

The time has come for the expression of creation to bring the truth to light. This is a time like no other, not since the spirit of God blew upon the wasteland of Earth and called the creatures into existence. Do you think that those who came before you always knew love? Not until consciousness was able to manifest that knowledge. Since manifestation and Source are a unit, love only made an appearance when universal consciousness was ready to accept it as part of itself. All expression has its origin in the being that gives it existence.

It would only be expected that once universal consciousness was able to accept love as part of what it is, conflict would arise. Remember that we refer to the consciousness of the material universe, not the infinite consciousness of God. When choosing to begin to express the love that is, this consciousness asked itself, what would that which it had manifested mean as part of what it is, being the opposite of love? How could it be possible to be two antagonistic things at the same time? This is how conflict entered the world. From that state of the soul, nothing could arise other than a kingdom of enmities and all kinds of rivalries. The growing conflict in the world bore witness to this. It could not be otherwise. Ultimately, those expressions allowed the universal consciousness to see the state of conflict it was in. It knew itself as what it was in the present. The contrasts were there in plain sight, so that it could know its own expressions. But love kept calling and it could no longer—nor did it wish—to ignore that voice.

That consciousness can observe itself is perhaps something obvious and not so transcendental. However, let me remind you that this was not always the case for the consciousness of the created. Before the moment of awareness, material creation was completely unconscious of itself. This includes humanity as well. Going from the state of unconsciousness to being aware of oneself has been a leap of immeasurable proportion. Only when your soul chose to be conscious and to abandon the state of unconsciousness could it jump into the light and let itself be embraced by love.

The question "What am I?" was not always visible in the consciousness of the created. The denial of being made it unable even to be consciously formulated. This is how she remained buried in the dark vaults of denial for as long as truth was denied, avoiding love's call to remain united with it forever. Unconsciousness is not a "state" properly speaking, although it is quite similar. It is actually a conscious condition in which the soul turns a deaf ear to God's call. By turning its back on the light of life, the perpetual sun on which existence is based, the soul could see only a shadow of itself projected. Believing himself to be that, he externalized darkness.

There came a time when you turned your gaze upon the truth. You were blinded by its luminescence at first, not having looked at it for so long. As your spiritual vision was restored you began to see with the eyes of Christ, the only source of true vision. When you sleep, your eyes are closed. When you wake up you keep them open. Something similar happens on the path of universal consciousness. From a dream state of forgetfulness, it moves to one of awakening to love. You know this well, but you rarely think about human nature as a whole, united to the whole of everything. This is not a play on words. It is the plain truth.

In unison, human nature fell into a long sleep; in unison it awakens. In the symbology of Genesis it was never said that Adam had awakened from his dream. However, that awakening is happening now.

IV. The Only Call

The time that elapsed between the moment when consciousness was immersed in the dream of Adam and the beginning of the awakening, was the time that preceded the first coming of Christ. Then the time of dreaming in exile ended, and a temporary space began in which universal creation began to awaken. To some extent, you can consider the incarnation of Christ in human form as the ringing of the bell of the Lord which resounded in all hearts, calling them to awaken to the reality of perfect love. Love was calling the soul in a new way, although with the same message and for the same purpose: to live eternally in the bliss of God's love. There never was another call; no other answer that love awaited.

Let me remind you of what we say here, given the importance it has for this revelation. Earthly life is but a time given to the soul to answer the question that Christ asks each being from the very moment of his creation. The time each takes to respond is a matter of freedom. But eventually everyone will respond.

I invite you to consider the time of the dream of oblivion not as a time in which being—knowledge, or God as you have conceived it up to now—has been denied. Rather, see it as a time when the soul still doubts before deciding. For that reason, love, in its infinite benevolence, has created the perfect universe where the soul is given the time it needs to decide by virtue of its free will. That request of the soul in unity with God is what created time itself, and with it, the world that you know with all its laws. That is also why, in the realm of time, love and truth live in all their beauty and holiness.

Daughter, son of my divine heart! Well-loved soul! You have never despised God, nor have you denied Her. In the holy exercise of your freedom you have simply asked for time to decide. Love approved your request. Therefore, God created for you a realm where that was possible, in unity with your free will and Her divine will, not as punishment, but so that together, holding each other in the light of unity, the truth of what that calling means will be revealed to you. And finally, you will make up your mind to accept love as your only reality, your source and endless joy, and truth as your holy abode, always united, always loving each other, always in the Heaven of love that has no beginning and no end.

3.

The Trumpets Sound

I. The Voice of Love

Once the call from Heaven became one with humanity in the incarnate Christ, the whole material universe began to hear it more clearly. It became one with the temporal dimension that the soul experiences. If you meditate on what is being said here, you will see that this makes sense.

If the call is universal, it cannot be absent in any reality that exists, even those not created by God. Even though the mind may want to manufacture a world of fantasy, the question of Christ will remain active in the soul of each being. Remember that thoughts are not being, nor are fantasies who you are; if they were, they would no longer be illusions, since what is attached to you becomes true because of who you are.

The call of Christ is universal and always active because it is the call into existence. Nothing would exist without it. And Mother-Father God knows that you and every creature want to exist, otherwise She would not have created them. God's creative action is not selfish. It does not arise from a divine will separate from the will of the created. By calling you to life, love has responded to your will to be.

God's call to creation is eternal, as is the soul's response. When the soul responds to the invitation of Heaven to live eternally in the happiness of the perfect love that it is, it does so in a perpetual way. Its endless answer does not mean you have to think about answering, or make eternal discernments, nor does it require words. Love does not think in terms of human thought. It does not reason elaborately. Love does nothing. Love just is. What else can God ask of the soul but the will to love, since that is all that is totally Hers?

The call that created your existence was not a divine whim; it was the result of your own will to be. How is it possible that before being created, you had already expressed your will to be? This is answered simply: You exist from all eternity because God is eternal. There never was a time when you and I did not exist united in the truth. Nor will there be.

How can one understand the truth that you have always existed, and your existence is the answer to your eternal will to be? The answer is to recognize the truth of who you are: an aspect of God. As such you must be eternal.

II. True Light Reflection

You are the mirror of Heaven in which God sees an aspect of Her being reflected. In other words, you are literally a little "piece" of Heaven. The infinite sum of all the mirrors of holiness—the various aspects of creation—is what enables God to know Herself in sonship. Can a creator know Herself as Creator other than through Her creations? If creation is the face of God, where She knows Her creative power, how could She not be holy, beautiful, and perfect?

In order for free will to exist, it was necessary that there be potential to turn one's back on truth. Obviously, if that option is taken, a state would arise in which, although creation is an expression of the divine, it could not be seen or recognized. But turning your back on the sun does not mean that the sun ceases to exist or that its rays stop embracing you with their light, warmth, and vitality. It only means that you are looking away, toward nowhere.

An easy way to understand this is the following. When you stopped looking at the truth as your only reality, what you did was leave your creative capacity in suspense, which is why the mind went blank. You did not stop being who you are, but the response to the invitation to be part of God's creative processes, to which you are called to join from the very moment of your creation, was suspended.

God is endless tenderness. This causes His will to arrange for His well-loved daughters and sons to be serenely and gently awakened. The wake-up call to love is softer than the faintest summer breeze, more tender than a beautiful snowflake. At the same time, it carries the power that creates life, and sustains the existence of the universe. Love always respects freedom. This is why everyone's timing and process to become conscious of and to respond to the invitation of love to live in the truth is respected. Heaven can wait because it knows that even in waiting there is love, holiness, and perfection. Respecting the freedom of the soul is an act of perfect love, and therefore holy.

In terms of the truth, it does not matter if you choose one path or another in relation to who you are. God will always be by your side and in you. God will continue to contemplate all glory as She contemplates you, because She sees no illusions. She sees everything as it is, the Source of being. Therefore, the wake-up call is not for Her, but for you. Why? So that you too can see the greatness, magnificence, and indescribable beauty of Christ, and thereby rejoice eternally in the joy of knowing yourself in Her.

What God sees when She looks at you leaves the soul speechless with love and beauty. In that perpetual vision of truth Her divine being lives in endless happiness, abundance, fullness without limits, love without borders. All that and much more—in terms of perfection—belongs to you by birthright. And what divine love wants you to make yours, is yours—and not only for you, but for all of creation. God calls all to live in the truth of the holiness that you are for all eternity. It is a call to live in peace that is the foundation of life without opposite.

III. The Choice of the Created

You are being clearly told, beloved of my heart, that what happened up to this moment, both for you and for the universal consciousness of the created, is that a path was traveled in time to be able to choose the fundamental option of the soul. It is also being revealed that that fundamental choice has been made by your soul and by all of creation. Simply put, to love, the created universe said "Yes." Therefore everything is being absorbed in it: lighting, gathering, sanctifying. As a result, the Age of Reason has been abandoned; the Age of the Heart begun. The history of creation has been a journey without distance from the state of being created, waiting to recognize the eternal option, to the moment when to Christ it says "Yes." Once this assent is done in the deep interior of consciousness, humanity lives its dark night of the soul, and then resuscitates in the light of life. As it is inside, so it is outside. As it happens in your way of being, it happens in the whole world.

Yes, my love! The time that preceded this new era called the Age of the Heart, which is manifesting now, has been a long road from the denial of being to the acceptance of it, then through the universal dark night, and from there to live in the light of divine glory. It could not be otherwise, since there are no essential differences between the part and the whole, between what each aspect of human nature is, and what the whole of humanity is.

At this point it is necessary to understand what we call the universal dark night. What you call the dark night, regardless of whether it refers to a soul or to the whole of creation—since both are a unit—refers to the time between the full acceptance of love as the only truth of being, to the undoing of what is not true. Once the various layers of illusion are dismantled, the sanctity of the being can shine forth in all its magnificence. To a certain extent, it is the birth of Christ in creation.

Before birth there is a process. Just as the life of an unborn child gestates in the darkness of the mother's womb, your being remains in the depths of the heart of Mother-Father God, protected from all deception, waiting for the perfect moment in which to emerge into the light. That perfect time is now—not an eternal now in the sense that it always could be, but a specific now: this historical moment of your life, of your soul, and of all creation, which of course includes the whole world. Now, and not before, in time. Wasn't that what time was created for? To give creation time to make the fundamental choice?

IV. The "Yes" Has Been Given

The universal call has been heard and answered. No one who hears it can stop responding, because listening and responding are essentially the same. In your consciousness and in that of creation, the time arrived when you decided to listen to the inner voice of love. When you made this choice, you gave your "yes" to Christ. By giving your "yes," you made the irrevocable decision that everything false about you and your reality would vanish forever. In other words, you asked the Holy Spirit to illuminate your humanity and undo everything not in harmony with the holiness of your being. And the Holy Spirit does not delay.

Immediately the Holy Spirit appeared in you and began to restore the memory of who you are to your mind and heart. To this end, you let yourself be carried into the desert where the Holy Spirit spoke to your heart, a dialogue in which not only your humanity participated, but all of creation: a dialogue from Father to son, from Mother to daughter, from loving teacher to humble and receptive student. It was a meeting of the whole, realized in the part. In that heart-to-heart encounter, everything was transformed. What never actually was, ceased to be forever. Thought structures, mental and emotional patterns, beliefs, ways of seeing things and ways of being, were at first replaced by their opposites in holiness, and finally completely abandoned.

As part of the transformation, your mind and heart were emptied of everything that you considered "yours" so that you could be absorbed by love. You stopped thinking as your small self and allowed Christ to think for you. You exchanged the desire to live for yourself for Christ to live in you. This happened not only to you, for it could not have arisen in your individual consciousness if that option was not already available. The time that preceded this real encounter with God was a time of preparation for the fundamental choice that you came to Earth to make.

The passage through time is the last step of the birth of being in which you are born into eternal life. This revelation is of great relevance, as it allows you to know the purpose of the world as

God sees it. Think of it not as a life given if you pass an exam or a series of tests, but as the last stage of the full realization of who you are. Those who came to Her came to wake up, and are ready to do so. Indeed, all who walk the paths of the world are awakening. In that sense everyone is awake, for they have come to the kingdom whose purpose is to awaken love.

How merciful God is, who allows the Kingdom of Time to exist, so that Her well-loved daughters and sons can choose love! How wise are Her works! She has provided everything necessary for the knowledge of truth to be gained through the exercise of freedom. How kind Her designs! She Herself has decreed the laws of the universe. In doing so, She endowed it with perfect laws so that the soul can know the truth about Her being. And by meeting in Her serene light, the soul gives a perpetual "yes" to the love of Christ. This is how the soul says "yes" to itself, for it is nothing but love. How great is love!

God's love is beyond all words. Her voice gave life to everything that lives. To creation She is mother and father, sister and brother, friend and companion. Her being is beyond any symbol; beyond human words. Being unlimited, She joins form to become one with matter. Being eternal, She embraces time. And all this for the pure love of the soul. In Her goodness She commands the angels to gently sound the trumpets of Heaven so that the whole universe can hear the voice of love, a heavenly song that will endure forever so that everyone can clearly hear the call from on high that says to each creature:

> *Come, My beloved, love of My being. Come and enjoy the wonders that I have prepared for you for all eternity.*

4.

Realization in Love

I. A New Age

Beloved of my being, pure soul! You may wonder why the Age of the Heart should begin to be lived now and not previously. What is the purpose of time? Why must you wait for the achievement of divine plans?

Time exists as an option within the pure potentiality of the soul; it could not have been conceived otherwise. Nothing can come into existence without the consent of the will of God, in accordance with His eternal laws. While what the Creator creates cannot be uncreated, what the mind fabricates in fantasy can be undone. No illusion is eternal. What is now happening is that the illusions that trapped creation, causing a whole system of limitation, are being dismantled.

An easier way to understand this is to realize that time is not moving forward as perceived, but backward. Time was stretched from eternity—the realm of no time—to a limit. Once it reached that limit, it began to withdraw. In reality, time is going nowhere, but given the tendency of the human mind to think in sequential terms, it will be helpful for the purpose of this dialogue to conceive of it that way. In the trajectory traveled by time, from eternity towards its maximum possible extension, the history of creation as you know it was manufactured, with humanity as a part.

We have said that time is going nowhere. This is something you can easily understand because time does not enter the sphere of space; they are different in nature, although they coexist within the same dimension. The same occurs with the various beings that populate the Earth: they are different, yet they share the same kingdom.

If time is going nowhere, it is not moving. If it doesn't move, how could it exist? Do you not think of it as something that slides from the present into the future, leaving a trail behind that you call the past? But if the future does not exist, and the past is not real, where can time "go" if the only real thing is the present? The answer is very simple: nowhere. Your "reality" exists only in the imagination.

The notion of time is one of the great universal beliefs passed from generation to generation, establishing itself in the human mind to the point that it seems impossible to conceive of existence without it. Daily life is governed by its apparent reality. It seems to encompass everything to such an extent that you cannot even conceive of the idea that it does not really exist.

II. Beginning to Remember

Returning to the Father's house is an expression that refers to a "return," to retrace one's steps back to a starting point. That is precisely what the physical universe is doing. It contracts until finally it returns to the state of perfect unity with eternity—the eternal present.

Time had separated itself from the realm of no time in order to try to know itself in the only way that it actually could not, that is, apart from the knowledge of God.

In the parable of the merciful father, the symbol of the prodigal son does not refer only to a person or soul. The son is the sonship, creation in its entirety, the universal consciousness of the created. The Father's house represents the Divine Kingdom, the only reality, whose laws are in harmony with what being—and thus creation—is in truth. It is impossible to live in peace outside of the Father's house, because there are no laws that allow such an existence, sustenance, or expression of being. Only within it can you be fully in the realm of reality. Like a fish out of water, you simply cannot go on living, because only the Kingdom of the water of life contains what is required to develop life to its fullness.

One of the reasons it is difficult for you to understand what is said here about time is that you know that love is expansion. Therefore the mind inquires, how can what is being said about the universe contracting be true if life is expansion? A temptation would be to say that in reality, the life of the world is not real and therefore it is not true life, so what is contracted is not life. However, this is incorrect. Earthly life is life because it is sustained by love. Otherwise, as we already said, it could not even be conceived. Furthermore, if the vital force of eternal life did not exist in it, Christ could never have joined with time.

Time's contraction occurs as the universe expands. If the universe expands enough, it reaches a point where it joins the eternal. The mind cannot understand or accept this through the intellect. Nevertheless, the mind united with the heart knows it to be true. Consciousness experiences this every time it joins with love. When love makes an appearance in your life, time collapses. And simultaneously you expand. You feel that you transcend all limits. You feel invulnerable, alive. This is not a mere perception; rather it comes from the memory of eternity. This memory, which arises from knowledge, lives in you and cannot be erased simply because it is who you are.

As part of universal creation, humanity is returning to the starting point, the Father's house. Humanity does this through its union with love. By joining love more and more, consciousness expands; and in that expansion, time, space, and matter as you have conceived of them are contracting. That is why I told you that your role was "to make you do nothing in love." In love you make yourself everything, while what is not true in you becomes nothing. This is also why I told you, "You give me nothing, and I give you everything back."

You might think of the limit of the extension of time as the lowest point reached in the fall of consciousness, or the maximum point of unconsciousness, after which the filiation began to become more and more aware of what it really is. Thus began the return to love, not because humanity hadn't been attached to love before, but because you had conceived of love as something other than yourselves.

III. Eternal Unity

It is not that the soul did not love the splendor of the Father's glory, or that His divine essence was not irrepressibly attractive, but when the soul contemplated it, she thought that the greatness of God was something other than her own being—admirable and venerable, but different.

The idea of a divine being separated from the soul is what created the world of duality. It is a realm in which doubt is possible for a time, a dimension in which love would coexist for a certain temporal space with the idea of an opposite to itself, so that the filiation can choose, not by a direct vision of truth, but indirectly through the opposites. Still, the call to choose would remain active even in dual consciousness. That appeal cannot be erased from the soul because it constitutes your being.

No matter where the filiation goes, whatever it does, or if it manufactures dimensions as it wishes, the call of love to remain in divine unity must accompany it always. The Kingdom of Heaven is the state of unity consciousness to which creation is united through the joyous acceptance of the divine call to live in the truth of what is—the happy recognition of being one with God. In this unity consciousness, the soul forever embraces the truth that in Him it is everything and enjoys all fullness, but outside of Him it is nothing because there is no reality outside of love—that God is love, just as the soul is. Therein lies unity: the union of love with love.

The universe expands because the consciousness that gives it existence expands. This is why it began with a point of matter in which the consciousness of the created on the physical plane condensed. From that starting point, which is actually the point of return to the consciousness of love, it began to expand more and more. This expansion was creating new beings, more and more consciousness, since they are the extensions of love. Remember that love always creates new love; the universe is expanding—so to speak—until it becomes one with the infinite. To return to the Father's house is to return to the consciousness of love.

All time and all limitation were contained in the initial point of matter. As universal consciousness expanded, time, matter, and also space became less dense, more subtle. The barriers between form and formlessness, between the manifested and the unmanifested, begin to disappear, as well as the barriers between the Source of everything created and creation, between God and you.

This is why the beings coming into existence in the universe now are more and more conscious and subtle, until the point will be reached when there is no difference between the Heavenly and the Earthly, the eternal and the temporal, and matter and spirit, as the will of God has always ordained. This explains why I spoke of the Alpha and the Omega. Everything arises from love and returns to love.

Since time itself is an illusion, you may wonder how it is possible for what does not exist to vanish. The answer is simple: illusions need time to exist and to vanish. Fantasies must retrace their steps over time to stop inhabiting the mind. The speed of retraction of fantasies is much faster than that of their development because the time to manufacture illusions proceeds vertically, not horizontally. You must climb the slope of separation, the denial of truth; but once you decide to return to love, you descend as if the soul loosened the ties that bound it to the world of illusion and jumped into the arms of love.

IV. Awakening to Love

Thus the undoing of the mental pattern of creating fantasies is carried out more rapidly and deeply, which is what humanity is experiencing in this time of transformation. Naturally, there is no actual "speed" as such, since time is going nowhere. What happens, rather, is that the thinking mind perceives changes it cannot quickly integrate through its learned reasoning. The learning mind is disoriented; the new cannot be comprehended using the old as a frame of reference. While you are still trying to integrate one change, you perceive another already happening, and so on. This creates a state of overwhelm for the mind. All this has a purpose: to finally stop believing the thinking mind and to put aside its learned interpretations of life.

Time is linked to cognitive memory and the ability to learn. Without memory, the mind could not learn, since there would be no "space" to store what was learned. This is what is normally called "world knowledge." However, when consciousness ceases to provide energy to that aspect of the mind and becomes detached from it, true knowledge from the mind of Christ, rather than from interpretations of a mind that tries to think by and for itself, begins to dawn. All this stimulates resistance from that aspect of the soul accustomed to conceiving of reality in its own way, and believing it should assign meaning to things.

As can be seen, what happens in the Earthly Kingdom is a process of undoing the mental, emotional, and other various patterns of the soul which vanish so you can be united with Christ in the fullness of being. This is humanity's "history of creation."

Once you accept love as your only reality and therefore what you are, the patterns described here are transmuted, one after another. The universe allows this to be done perfectly and in peace, not just for you but for all of creation, because the consciousness of love encompasses universal consciousness within itself. In other words, physical creation, the world and your existence, collaborate with your will and God's will to live consciously united in the bliss of perfect love—for you and for all of creation.

Trusting that God will bring fulfillment to a happy end to you and to all is to live in the truth. In your being is the knowing that this is true. You know that life is in the hands of a Supreme Being who gives it its existence and sustains it with benevolence through the vital force of pure holy love. This knowledge, which comes from your perfect knowledge of God, abides within you. You can access it every moment. In order for that beauty to shine in your mind and heart, you need only quiet your soul a little. In this way you invoke peace and allow the voice of love to be heard by you and by all. In doing so, you become aware of the Sacred Heart from whose beating springs the life of your being, and in whose love you dwell eternally, in unity with everything.

Soul full of light! Heart full of beauty! Understand well that the purpose of time and everything attached to it is to take you gently into the realm of no-time. Once within its doors, time vanishes forever and returns to the formless, boundless reality of the Holy Spirit. On that threshold of Heaven, God Herself takes your hand, kisses your soul, and with all sweetness tells you:

My love, daughter, son of my divinity, welcome Home.
I was waiting for you. Come, enjoy the delights of my love which
have belonged to you forever. Yours is Heaven, yours is the land,
yours are the angels, and yours is My heart,
because Christ is yours and is everything for you.

And you melt forever in love.

5.

The Seven Waves of Consciousness

I. The Return Begins

Beloved incarnation of Christ, soul born of my Divine Love! Thank you for giving me your attention, time, and humanity to unite us in the truth and holiness of who we are. In our direct relationship dwells the wisdom of Heaven, perfect knowledge, and endless joy. What happiness our hearts experience in being together in this dialogue! What deep serenity comes to the mind with the assured knowing of Christ!

My love, once we have traveled towards the loving understanding of the path of the soul and the universal consciousness of the created, it is necessary to realize that the journey of creation goes from a maximum state of lack of unity with truth towards union with it. You already know that the truth is Christ. Therefore, in this work both expressions—truth and Christ—will be treated synonymously, since they are two ways of expressing the same indescribable reality.

In order to more easily understand this, we will use the example of Earth. In its origins, its union with the consciousness of Christ was practically non-existent. We say "practically," because strictly speaking nothing can exist without the spark of reality that gives it existence, which comes from our Mother-Father God. However, existing and being are not the same. For the purposes of these writings, we will consider "existing" as everything that exists but is not fully aware of its union with the Source of being. "Being" refers to everything that exists and that is aware of the love that life and its existence give it.

It is fair to make this distinction, since life without love is purposeless—a restricted, limited life devoid of creative power. It is not a complete life, nor is it eternal. In this sense, and only in this sense, can we say that it is not life. But life lived in love has a holy purpose. It creates new love, divine extensions, and is forever limitless. How could it be otherwise if love is the foundation, source, reality, and destiny of life?

The time that elapsed between the manifestation of shapeless mass from which the entire material realm emerged and the appearance of form was the first wave of consciousness, the first step, so to speak, towards the return to the House of Truth. A shapeless thing took shape. Planets, galaxies, and beautiful constellations appeared. The moon and stars began to shine in beauty. Thus was born the universe that you contemplate today. You may not consider what a leap in consciousness like this meant, since you tend to take for granted that what you perceive has been there forever. But although they existed in the sheer potentiality of consciousness, they did not manifest themselves until it was their time to be. Everything in the realm of time has its time.

II. A New Step Towards the Truth

Let us now consider what happened on Earth. Step by step it began to be populated with more and more conscious beings. The time that elapsed from the existence of the barren land until the manifestation of conscious life in its environment constitutes the second wave of the movement of consciousness towards the full realization of the unity of the created with Christ, the journey back to truth. In that age, beings lacked awareness of themselves, but they could recognize—albeit to a limited extent—that creation existed. This was an immense leap. Consciousness began to expand more and more, now including the awareness that a universe existed. It continued moving slowly but surely towards awakening to love, to the consciousness of oneness.

Beloved daughter, son, listen with an open heart to the next part of the story. The extension of the material universe, the history of creation, is a movement of expansion of consciousness. Its purpose is your reintegration into the whole. This journey consists of seven waves of consciousness, from an unconscious state—the maximum degree of separation or condensation allowed—towards a reunion with love, that is, with Christ.

Consciousness never stops expanding, advancing towards the infinite vastness of the heart of God. Still, in the consciousness of the physical universe there are quantum leaps in which it extends further than in its previous trajectory—something like a universal leap of consciousness. Each one of these jumps is what we call a "wave" of consciousness. Let us follow this path together.

The third wave covers the time from the awareness of conscious life in its created environment, but not of itself, to the appearance of a self-aware being. This new manifestation of consciousness is called humanity. Its purpose is to reunite physical creation with God. For this it has been created. Its nature has been endowed with everything necessary for the divine plan to be fulfilled perfectly.

Thus once creation was ready, the sons and daughters of our Mother-Father God were present in humanity. First it was an expression without language as you know it, and an almost non-existent degree of awareness of its humanity, much less of its union with Source. Creation had to wait a while before seeing human nature with more consciousness.

III. The Memory of God

We will give the name "fourth wave" to the period from the existence of a humanity conscious of itself and of creation but unconscious of the existence of God, to the appearance of a religious being, one capable of being aware of the existence of a Supreme Being as the origin, lord, and destiny of life, and of expressing a relationship with this.

At this time, religions and religious institutions emerged, along with knowledge of the truth as you know it. Creation began to witness the first cities, nations, and currents of philosophical and transcendent knowledge as a natural expression of that state of consciousness. God began to be recognized, was given a name, a symbol, and a house in which to be worshipped. This was still a separate "god" from creation, however.

We have said "god" with a small letter, because that was not the true God. It was a first approach towards the recognition of divine essence, existence, and reality. There was a God, but as distant from creation as the stars in the sky, and even much more. Still, humanity placed God in Heaven. As such, that conception was perfect, for it ushered in the next stage of consciousness.

This is how the universe of time and form began to become self-aware: it was accomplished through a humanity capable of considering the question, "What am I?" More precisely, the fundamental question was present in consciousness. For this reason, creation would be reunited with Christ, since in that question the voice of love resounds, calling the soul to live eternally in its divine reality.

We call the fifth wave the period of time that goes from the appearance of humanity, conscious of creation, itself, and God, up to the manifestation of a being capable of conceiving the one God as united with the created, which invariably leads to the recognition of the God of love. This is the First Advent. In this fifth wave of consciousness, Christ becomes humanity and thus gathers everything created in himself. There is no need to elaborate on this as you know its effects well, and much has already been said of it. However, we will say that from that moment in the history of creation a new era commenced, the era of the humanized Christ. We call this the sixth wave of consciousness.

IV. The Humanized Christ

Graceful soul, the sixth wave of consciousness is the time in which you are now living. It includes the time from the resurrection of Jesus Christ until the full realization of deified humanity.

This sixth age of consciousness represents human nature manifesting as an expression of Mother-Father God. Once accomplished, it remains united within itself in all of creation— the humanized Christ manifested in each human. Simply put, humanity, reunited with love, will cause all creation to reunite in it. How is this possible? It is easily understood. Remember that what you join becomes holy because of who you are, just as love is created by virtue of your being. This has always been the case, as it is in me. My union with you made you one with my divine being. In the same way, your union with creation will reunite it with the love that we are together in unity.

In this sixth age of consciousness, the humanized Christ ceases to be an individual being separate from others, and is recognized for what you are: the living expression of what every human being is in truth, and with it, every aspect of holy creation.

Daughter, son of light, let me remind you of a few things. Since God is known in love, creation could not enjoy the glory of the Mother-Father while immersed in totally fearful consciousness, which is unconsciousness. That is why it was necessary to create time. Time arose as an effect of the contraction of consciousness, the limitation caused by the denial of being. However, love could never allow something to exist that prevents the living into the truth of itself if it so disposes. Therefore, the kingdom of time carries within itself that which allows the created to grow towards its reality and foundation, the awareness of truth and love. Once achieved, the way to the Kingdom of Heaven would be clear again in universal consciousness.

The present era—what we have called the sixth wave of consciousness—is the prelude to the new Heaven and the new Earth. This is what creation is about—not just the Earth, but everything that exists in the physical universe. Remember, my beloved, that the history of creation is but a journey without distance from the darkness of forgetting the Christ of your being toward the light of the memory of Christ, and from there to full union. In that union, you are one with God, that is, with love.

V. A New Heaven and A New Earth

Let us now take the final step in understanding what is revealed in this dialogue. The seventh and last wave of consciousness is the era that arises as an effect of the current one, a state in which creation consciously lives as the unity that it is with God. In such a kingdom, humanity—and with it creation—not only knows that there is a God who is love and becomes one with it, but consciously lives as the expression of Christ in truth—that is, as the son or daughter of Mother-Father God who always was and will always be. In short, the consciousness of the filiation returns to the truth of what it is.

The expression "a new Heaven and a new Earth" implies that the entirety of creation will live in the unity of Spirit. Time and eternity will be one, just as they always have been. Everything will live in the love that God is. No aspect of the sonship will be excluded, nor can it exclude itself, for the knowledge of truth will be restored forever in the consciousness of creation.

Naturally, child of my heart, blessed soul, we will not focus our dialogues on the ages past or the one to come, but on the present, the reality that humanity is living now. We have traveled a path of the revelation of how consciousness is creating effects according to what it is. This was necessary so that there is no doubt that everything that happens in the life of the world, and in yours in particular, is but the result of the consciousness that gives rise to it.

From a humanity conscious of the truth of the love that is, a very different world arises than from one born in the shadow of fear and unconsciousness. Does this not make sense? You have already experienced a turnaround in your life at some point. There was a "before" and an "after" for you. Why? Because in the depth of your being you said "yes" to Christ. In doing so, everything changed. You began to bear witness to the truth with your way of being, acting, and expressing yourself. At first it seemed pretty messy and lacking harmonic consistency. But little by little it took shape until it was a clearly defined, consistent, and increasingly beautiful expression.

Your human aspects accommodate to become the expression of the consciousness that gives it existence. This has always been the case; human nature is the servant of spirit. But when a servant serves two masters, he cannot serve either well, nor in a clear and serene way, especially when they are diametrically opposite in every way.

When you placed your humanity in service to love, even without the thinking mind being able to understand it clearly at first, conflict ceased. All the mind's strengths and abilities began to join in. This is how you rejoined love. After being reunited with love, your expression could not help but be what love is. Before that, you expressed what was in harmony with the state of consciousness you were in—a conflicted, divided consciousness. A unified consciousness extends unity and eliminates conflict and division. This is true not only for you, blessed soul, born of my dear love, but for everything that exists. Be glad that this is so.

6.

The Time of Peace

I. Times of Fullness

Holy soul, creature of light, now that you know that humanity, as part of creation, has been making a journey without distance from the maximum allowed unconsciousness towards full consciousness of unity with Christ, that is, with the whole, we are in a position to speak of what will be part of the world from now until the advent of the new Earthly Kingdom.

Why do this? So that our brothers and sisters can know and leave behind the uncertainty in which many would find themselves without the existence of this work. Without this revelation, many would rush to discouragement, and others to despair, because the changes that will unfold will seem more and more rapid, profound, and confusing. However, as I have promised, I will be with you until the end of the world. Remember, my beloved, that love will never leave you.

Creation has entered the final phase of time prior to awareness of the fullness of love. In other words, you are entering the age of consciousness of the reunion in Christ of all creation. As a result, there will only be room for what comes from love; everything else will be dismantled more and more quickly. Unity will be the hallmark of this phase which we call the Age of the Heart. You may wonder why we chose such a name. Answering this question is the purpose of these words that Heaven gives to everyone out of love.

The Age of the Heart is an age in which humanity will live more and more centered on being, understood as the union of reason and love, mind and heart, human and divine nature. This means that the more subtle capacities of the soul will be revealed as an expression of the indwelling Holy Spirit. Intuition, sensitivity, knowing it is not of the world and yet perfect, the ability to love all things in God, and many other characteristics coming from perfect charity which have not yet been displayed collectively by humanity, will begin to manifest. There will simply be no room for systems based on the rational mind separated from love and compassion. They will find no means to continue to exist, nor will emotions that are disconnected from reason.

Those souls who understand that love, and only love, is what will rule the time of creation from now on and until its fullness in Christ will save themselves great suffering. This is because the universe has been created with corresponding laws that support what is part of truth. That is, creation carries within itself laws that sustain the being of pure love that each created thing is in truth. The rest, what is not love, has no law to support it. Accordingly it will fade. It has always been this way. The difference is that now what is not love will no longer return to restart a loveless cycle. Beginning in these times, everything that vanishes because it is alien to love will never return. The wind of infinite mercy will carry it away, to be burned in the fiery furnace of divine love.

Systems not anchored in love, and therefore not in truth, will crumble. This includes everything that structures the life of the world: families and their structures; the laws and morality of humans; their vision of the universe; their understanding of life; relationships between brothers and sisters and with nature. The list goes on until the entirety of what humanity has reflected so far is complete. Finally peace will reign in all hearts, and, as an effect of it, on Earth. The conclusion of the sixth wave of consciousness is peace, which will immediately give way to love.

II. Harmony: The Reality of Truth

In order for the peace of Heaven to enter the abode of the soul, it must first be purified. Otherwise, there would be no harmony. Then love enters by itself. That is why the Age of the Heart is characterized by an insistent call to live in peace. Truly, the presence of peace in your lives will bring you the treasures of the Kingdom. That is why I extend my invitation to all humanity to do everything in your power—in union with my Sacred Heart and the Immaculate Heart of Mary—to remain in peace.

Peace is the calling and sign of the Age of the Heart. I invite you to meditate on it. In truth, I tell you that you will see more and more manifestations of searches for peace, longings for peace, spaces for peace. It will be the great transformer of creation. Peace does not come alone but with all of Heaven, for she is the spouse of the Holy Spirit.

What you are being told is that the era of the Holy Spirit is over, and now the Age of Peace has begun. The Holy Spirit came to put the house in order. Peace came to calm hearts and fill them with light, so that love may make an appearance in all its glory and splendor. Let me say this another way: Jesus has given you the Holy Spirit, which has given you Mary, mother of all creation and Queen of Peace. She will give you Christ again—no longer as a being that emanates from her blessed womb, but in everything created.

Divine Motherhood will be made fruitful by the hand of peace. As a result of this, Christ will shine in everything; divine light cannot be hidden. Happy are they who understand this sweet truth. They will live with the serenity that comes from certainty of purpose. Their minds will be still and receive answers to their questions. And their hearts will overflow with joy.

What is united will remain; what is divided will succumb. This eternal truth has been unequivocally manifested throughout human history. Now, however, it will take on a new force. The union will now be one of love. Any other type of union will be destined to disappear because the Age of the Heart has no room for anything other than the direct experience of truth. And the truth is that love is union—not because one is the cause of the other, but because they are the same.

Nations that do not seek unity will disappear. Laws that do not reflect equality before the truth will cease to apply because they will not be followed or supported. Even the jobs of men and women around the world with companies or industries that do not extend equality in love, will not survive.

III. The Expression of Unity

You may be wondering how all this will come about. The answer is that since human life is a manifestation of its consciousness, the hearts of sons and daughters of light who are already here and will continue to arrive and inhabit the Earth will not tolerate anything incapable of creating harmony, peace, and happiness in their lives. Such will be the preponderant criteria of the men and women who will walk the Earth. As a consequence, systems will have to adapt.

This is how the Spirit of Peace is co-creating the new Earthly Kingdom with humanity.

You may argue that humanity has always been seeking happiness, albeit in different ways and with different challenges. However, the harmony, joy, and peace that will be sought in the Age of the Heart will be linked to the perfect knowledge of Christ. This means that the search, although it may appear to be the same, will not be identical. Different efforts, even if named the same, do not create the same effects. Remember, my sons and daughters, that form cannot cause content to cease being what it is. We could affirm with certainty that the searches for fulfillment and survival, even those for the improvement of quality of life and other similar lives, although their purpose was to create a happier world, could not help being embedded in a disconnected human-centric idea of the unity of God.

A humanity over here and a divinity over there has been the way of perceiving and understanding life as consciousness passed from one wave to another in its awakening to love. I assure you, pure soul, that the effects of living in unity are very different from those of living in separation. For the purposes of truth, what has happened along the path of creation is that it has gone from not recognizing God to recognizing God's existence as separate from human reality. Now that changes forever.

If you listen carefully and calmly to what is being said, you can see that the gap of separation has been narrowing, wave after wave, until it reached the current point where humanity is ready to live in unity with Christ—or more precisely, to accept that unity is the only reality. To live united in God is to live sensibly, because there you dwell in reality. When the mind and heart are disconnected from reality, there is endless disharmony because no laws can support what is not real. Everything disengaged from love is madness precisely because it has no foundation in reality. This truth will be fully recognized.

Living without God has been the way of humanity until the Age of the Heart. This statement may seem a bit of an exaggeration since you think that humanity has venerated and praised God for many centuries. That is true to some extent, but not fully.

The God that humankind has hitherto known and whom many have worshiped was not the true God because none of them have been the Mother-Father God of love. It could not be otherwise, according to the state of consciousness then existing. However, past ages gave rise to the present one, each like a link of light that allowed humanity to stay united to the source of truth. Step by step, creation returns to love. This allows us to understand, beloved of my divine being, that it is not necessary to examine or judge the past. Everything contributed to our being here, you and I united and embraced in the unity of everything created and its Source.

When the light of life makes an appearance in creation, it does so through very concrete beings. They are part of the plan of restoration of the consciousness of the created. This work, although it seems something that reaches but a few minds and hearts—since every written work reaches a minuscule number of beings compared to the totality of creation—is nevertheless a beam of light of consciousness expanding throughout the universe. These words manifested here are the expression of a universal state of consciousness. By bringing them into expression, the whole of creation receives them. They could not have been written a single instant previously, nor after this time. By such, I do not mean only the writing itself but the reception of it.

IV. Heaven Is Here

Beloved of my divine heart, this work has been written from the realm of no-time for each one of you who receive it in time. By welcoming it with love and openness of heart, you extend it into universal consciousness. Your "yes" to love has brought you together with divine power. Because of this, a power that is beyond all possible worldly understanding and imagination flows from the source of eternal life to you, and from your center to all created things. Together we are opening consciousness so the light of Christ shines as never before in the world. You will see how it grows and grows until it becomes a radiant sun which no one can fail to recognize as the source of their being.

Become one with the peace of God. Do not look for anything else. In it you will obtain not only the treasures of the Kingdom, but everything necessary for the new Earthly Kingdom to shine in all its beauty and holiness. Never forget that peace is the calling and sign of the Age of the Heart, which has already begun in humanity. Trust in its benevolence, in its divine power, and in its holy face. It, and only it, will bring love in all its breadth to dwell forever on Earth as it is in Heaven.

The Age of the Heart will not be based on intellectual flow. That path, which was called the Age of Reason, has just ended to give way to these new times in which the unity of the soul will express itself as never before. It will bear witness to the union of mind and heart in perfect unity with Christ. What can be deduced through mental learning will not occupy the central place it previously did, although it will be valuable as long as it serves to manifest love.

In the peace of God you will find the eternal wisdom that lives in your being. And you will act from it. For this reason it is fair to say that the Age of the Heart will be an age of the wise, not the learned; of divine lovers, not of romantics; a time in which the divine Spirit will be heard in the depths of each soul without interference. Out of it the new Heaven and the new Earth will emerge in due time.

I can never emphasize enough the importance of staying in peace. When you create an inner space to welcome peace, you are expanding universal consciousness. This enlargement allows creation to reach a greater knowledge of the love of God, and with it, to live in the truth.

Can you now realize the importance of peace? Through it, not only do you feel better about yourself, but you renew the Earth and allow the love of Christ to flow from divine being into creation. I ask you with humility and gentleness to make peace your only treasure. Give it your hearts. Give the sweet presence of it to every step you walk. Take it wherever you go so that it can heal the hearts that still need healing, clarify the minds still asleep in the dream of oblivion, and expand any consciousness not yet open to the eternal novelty of love.

Embrace the mystery so that the breadth of your minds and hearts, always united to Mother-Father God, can touch the truth. For this it is necessary to live in peace. Disharmony causes confusion and leads the soul to the terrain of conflict, all of which prevents its full attention to what sustains its reality, the truth of what it is. Truly, truly, I tell you that the new will be born of peace.

7.

Spirit of Communion

I. In the Divine Relationship

Beloved, blessed soul, light that illuminates the world! What a joy it is to spend time in unity with truth! How much joy our hearts experience, united in holiness, every time we enter into these sacred dialogues, which unfold in the most holy temple of our unity!

If you stop to meditate on the gift of these words, bliss would be your natural response. Not for the content they bring, nor for the symbols and expressions, but because every moment you spend alone with me in meeting this work—reading, absorbing, feeling, meditating, savoring the presence of a knowledge that is not of the world but is manifested in it—each time you do so, your consciousness of oneness widens. Universal consciousness opens for each of you.

Do not forget that the part and the whole are a unit, and that your spiritual growth brings about growth in all creation. Nothing is harmful in your spirit, because life resides there, and life is never sterile. Life always bears fruit, and in abundance.

Truly I tell you that a communion of souls exists. You have already experienced that; you have all had at least a glimpse of what this means. Perhaps it was a flash of unity, expressed as a feeling of meeting someone—apparently unknown—and feeling that you knew each other even before seeing each other physically. Maybe you perceived that but the other person did not, or both felt it in unison. Or perhaps you have had the experience of the communion of spirit through what you call synchronicities—events that happen in such a way that you become aware of a divine direction behind them. Or you have experienced a feeling that someone is calling you from somewhere far away. All these experiences, and many others, are a small glimpse of the communion that exists between all created souls and creation itself.

Everything is united. Nothing is separate. This is the truth of the Age of the Heart. Souls will increasingly live in a state of communion, which you could say is characteristic of this new era of consciousness. As a result there will be more and more unions of disembodied love, that is, unions that are not based on physical aspects as was customary.

The body will fulfill its function as it must according to the purpose of the Holy Spirit. It will be a means of communication of beings of pure love, whom it will represent in a perfect way. Unions based on love will be real. There will be no need for some to seek benefits from others. Love that floods hearts knows nothing of such things; those who live in love, and who will be more and more, will not even think in terms of uses and benefits. Their ways of discerning and deciding will be based on what allows them to live in the peace that their souls have known eternally. What does not bring peace to the heart or what brings suffering will be discarded.

Peace and happiness are heralds of love, eternal companions that never part. What comes from Christ cannot be disunited; all of the treasures and virtues of Christ remain in the unity of truth. This is why when you die in the peace of God, all the gifts of divine love are given to you without limitation. Seek peace and you get life. Abide in love and you give life. All this is well known to the soul. Otherwise, how could it be put into words in this work?

II. The Purpose of Returning

Remember, sacred soul, you who receive these words, that time is not advancing but regressing, taking the universe back to the eternal truth in which we all dwell in perfect unity, harmony, and holiness. Returning to the point where this truth dwells, which has never been eliminated from the soul, is what the becoming of time is all about. Once in truth, time will no longer be perceived as it currently is. It will simply no longer exist in the mind or in the heart. It will return to amorphous timeless eternity.

Can time disappear and still the life of the physical universe as it is known today continue? Of course. To believe that the universe cannot be resignified by love, making the perfect trinity of time, space, and matter something new, is to not comprehend the infinite power of being.

The difference between the universe of separation and the new Earthly Kingdom lies in the fact that in the first, everything served the purpose of accomplishing a return to unity. This supposes that the created was not in it. Therefore, everything in that holy and blessed universe, so full of beauty and vastness, had to make use of separation to bring everyone back to union. In other words, it had to use wrong perception to bring all to holy perception.

The new Earthly realm will no longer require time, space, and matter to be used by spirit to return to unity. So what role will time, space, and matter play in it? You have been told correctly, though not exactly, that those three dimensions of the physical universe were mechanisms of separation, each separating in a different way. This was true within the will to live in separation. But it was not, nor is it, the essence of creation. Using things for which they were not created has been the basis of times past. It might be said that this has been the philosopher's stone upon which the world's thought system was built: giving things a meaning that love would never have given them. This has been the course in which humanity has been trapped, but those times will not continue.

In the Age of the Heart, time, space, and matter will be used for the purpose for which they were created: to express love. Everything will converge in love.

Remember—and this reminder is essential to this work—that love does not destroy but makes all things new. In this truth resides the peace that is needed to walk the path of life here and now. Think not, my daughters and sons, that this is of little relevance, for fear of life's destructiveness has gripped human hearts. Letting go is necessary in order to dwell in the truth.

III. The Inheritance of Peace

What is the point of believing that God will destroy all things to create something new, if all things belong to Him? Is the fact that you made an improper use of creation a reason for its destruction?

Beloveds from all corners of the world, daughters and sons of my divine heart! The world will not perish. The catastrophes of which you have heard so many times will not happen. Love watches over everything and everyone. The consciousness of humanity is increasingly anchored in Christ. This means that present and future humanity are not exactly the same humanity that once walked the Earth. I assure you that you will find the way to live in peace. You will do it because we will do it together, united in the sanctity of our direct relationship, the hallmark of the Age of the Heart.

Naturally, in a world where the spirit of communion will increasingly manifest itself, words will become increasingly scarce, and will come to have another purpose. People will communicate heart to heart, not only with each other but also with the other beings of creation, which will allow holy relationships to exist everywhere. Indeed, this will be the rule of relationship in this age leading up to the new Earthly Kingdom. No relationship will be untouched by the sixth wave of consciousness in which humanity is now. I invite you not to judge new relationships through the prism of the ones you knew in the past, for if you do so you will be unable to understand them and they will engender fear.

The fundamental basis of relationship in this blessed era that has begun will be the authenticity of the heart. That which does not arise from love and is therefore not part of the truth—the hidden, the unsaid, the disguised, and the merely acted—will cease to exist.

When will this come about, you may wonder? My answer: it is already here. You are fully immersed in the age of Christ, the end times toward the fullness of love. I assure you, you are living in a golden age, full of heavenly graces, a phase in the history of creation without comparison. You have started the Age of the Heart, an era that has come as a response to humanity's longing for love, the echo of what creation cries for from its depths of being.

Unity and communion are synonymous. Increasingly, you will witness the reality of the common union that exists among you and with all creation. As you become more aware of it, the links will change as well as the relationship with the Earth and all things. This will be the natural effect of a change in your relationship with yourself. You will cease to think of man or woman as the epicenter of the universe of consciousness. You will realize that the center of the universe is the consciousness of oneness in which all dwell, embraced in love with everything created in perfect harmony.

You will also witness the physical world as a simple expression of who you are. You will know that you can continue expressing yourself in it as much as you want, or stop doing so, as you decide. Your choice will not change who you are and what all of God's creations are: full beings who know Heaven, the source of all life, being, and fullness.

IV. The Awake Universe

The world will see Christ as never before. I assure you. This vision will make everything change the way of understanding life, things, and the affairs of existence. Eternal truth—that which was once seen indirectly through the eyes of faith—will soon be seen and heard through the senses of spirit, just as it was in the beginning. There have always been those who have had this experience, from the third wave of consciousness to the present.

There are many more of these than you could count because they belong to all created kingdoms, not just humanity. They will grow in number day by day. New generations will come into the world with that knowledge imprinted in their minds and hearts and they will carry it in their conscious awareness. The vision of Christ can never be lost by them, for they are the living expressions of the Second Coming, the perfect prelude to the new Earthly Kingdom.

Just as peace will be the signature and seal of the Age of the Heart, unity will be its foundation. In effect, one will call the other. In a world of unions based on love, where it is recognized that everyone remains within the embrace of Christ, and that this is the reality of life, there can be no room for division, war, or the desire to be special. And there won't be. The decisions of the people, and the way in which the Earth will adjust to this new era of consciousness, will demonstrate the truth of this. Day after day you will see more signs of holiness, inclusion, and appreciation of others for the simple reason that this is life manifested. Life will be back in its rightful first place. Nothing will be above it, for Christ will be increasingly reflected in creation.

Even the systems of production, work, and government will be transformed in this new world that we call the Age of the Heart. Only those in service to love will persist—those who contribute to an authentic common good, demonstrate equality of life, respect diversity and uniqueness, and do so collaboratively in holiness. Collaboration will be the natural effect of the spirit of communion.

V. The Grace of Union

Do not forget, my beloveds, that creation is unity. Therefore collaboration among brothers and sisters will be their expression. Even collaboration itself will be transformed, for until now, humanity has known a limited form of collaboration, since it did not fully include everyone, everything, all creation, and God in it. But it will.

Universal consciousness is in a perfect position to bear witness to unity as never before. The way of Christ will be carried out in all creation, not as historical reality, but as the expression of consciousness. What served the past will not serve the present nor the future. This is how new the new creation is. But be aware that love will not abandon anyone or anything. It will not leave you without answers or perfect knowledge to walk the blessed paths of life.

The angels of God are already stationed everywhere on Earth. There are so many you could not count them. They will guide you just as my love for humanity will. Fear nothing; success is assured. The threshold that separated one era from the next has already been crossed. You have entered the era of the Sacred Heart. Together we will continue to walk in the light, hand-in-hand, talking, loving each other, expressing ourselves, and savoring the truth. United we will call all of creation to bear witness to the sanctity of life. And Christ will shine forth with glory, in whose beauty God's creation dwells.

Blessed are you who listen to my voice and follow it! Love will remain in your hearts every day of your life. Your minds will rest in peace. And your joy will be great.

8.

From the Idea to the Relationship

I. In the Embrace of Truth

Beloveds of Heaven, daughters and sons of my divine being! Here we are again, you and I, united in the sanctity of our reality. We are one. We are the eternal oneness of love. There is no other relationship like ours in the entire universe. From it emerges divine power in all its magnificence. Perhaps few realize how powerful this relationship with Christ is, in whose unity resides Heaven, Earth, and all that is created in utmost perfection.

What a joy it is to remain within the dialogue of love! How much beauty radiates from this manifestation, born of our holy love! We are moved by love. We are encouraged by truth. We reach our fullness by giving ourselves. Therefore we are witnessing what happens between you and me: we not only extend love from my being to yours and from your beauty to mine, but we also include the entire universe within these dialogues. No one is excluded from the embrace of our union, for we are one mind, one holy heart, one truth. United we are wisdom radiating to the entire world.

These words will go where they need to go. Everything is accomplished. Recall that time does not advance towards nothingness, but returns to the holy abode of truth. I assure you that no soul that has been part of the design of this manifestation will fail to receive these words. Some will even receive them without being fully aware of it. Think not about how this will be accomplished, for that is a matter for the Holy Spirit, who is the carrier, origin, and fulfillment of our holiness.

In this meeting of the sacred and the human, of the totality that we are, I come to reveal to you how in the Age of the Heart the idea of God gives way to a direct relationship with Her. As we have already noted, the Universe has carried out—and continues to carry out—a path towards the realization of truth, towards the pure consciousness of perfect love, origin, and purpose of all things, including you and the entire world.

II. Mysticism and Reality

Until very recently, humanity had only reached a stage where it could conceive of the idea of God, though that included something quite sublime that approached the truth. However, any concept of God is inaccurate and incomplete because of the limitation of thought. Nobody and nothing can define the Divine Being, Source of all life and virtue, just as it is impossible to define what you really are. Being cannot be limited. Concepts have borders; love does not.

To express universal consciousness, what next step can humanity take but to move toward a direct relationship with Mother-Father God? None, since the natural path of knowledge goes from a state of knowing indirectly through the intellect, to knowing directly, through the whole being. Mystical experiences once reserved for the few able to see the light of life will now become more like common currency. More and more people will see Christ face to face and will be living witnesses to spiritual reality, as were the ancient mystics, sages, and teachers.

Integrating the living experience of a direct relationship with God will be the central feature of what might be called a time of transition between the abandonment of the Age of Reason and the full establishment of the Age of the Heart. Naturally it takes time to go from a state in which you think about God to that of living in unity with Her, since this change involves all human and universal reality.

A direct relationship with God transmutes all things, including the minds, hearts, and bodies of the ones who have the experience of the unitive relationship. From there it spreads out into the universe. Remember, a leap in consciousness in humanity comes about in unison with all creation. This is why we say that this work, having been co-created with all the minds and hearts that exist in creation, opens the floodgates of a new universal consciousness.

Think about the following, my child. Give me the beauty of your memory and imagination. When you enjoy a beautiful musical work, you are there. You taste it, feel its beauty, join with it, and let yourself be carried away by its melody. Now consider: does that music exist only because of the performing musicians? Are they its origin and its end? Obviously not—the music exists because there were countless beings involved, and countless events that had to happen one after another for it to finally exist in consciousness and be heard, felt, and loved by your humanity. No created work is carried out but in unity because God is union, since God is love.

If God is union, and I assure you that this is true, how else is it possible to know God but through union? The unitive relationship with Christ is the goal of time and of all that exists in the material universe, for in it all that is true exists in perfect harmony with the sanctity of divine creation. In other words, everything that exists works together to bring you, everyone, and everything into the arms of love. Resting in love is the longing of your soul and of all creation, and the only thing perfectly certain to happen as the final outcome of time.

III. Everything Serves Love

We speak of dwelling every day of your life in the love that you really are. That is what the history of creation is about: returning to the arms of love. Bringing that into full realization is a collaborative endeavor. For this you have come into the world. Your way of being— your consciousness or human form united with what you are— is perfect to accomplish this, and that is how each fulfills the purpose of God in the world and in the Kingdom of Heaven.

In other words, you come into the world to save yourself and others, including me, your divine love and Creator. You come to wake up to love and awaken together with countless living beings who remain eternally united to you in me. As my heart has always known, "together they fell asleep in my arms, and together they will wake up." I am the one who sees everything, knows everything, and includes everything in love.

Perhaps your thinking mind wonders, how is it possible that God has to be saved? How can it be true that you are the one who saves me, that I am the Christ in you, and therefore the only and true Christ of God? In love and holiness we will answer that question together.

If you do not love yourself, if you do not live in the freedom of the sons and daughters of Mother-Father God in harmony with the being that you really are as has been arranged from all eternity, then what I am in you is imprisoned since you cannot express yourself. Perfect love stops being extended in your uniqueness. Remember, only you can love in your own way. No one can love for another, or make another love him or her. Your unique and unrepeatable way of loving is inextricably linked to who you are; there is no distinction between you and your loving. Loving and being love are one, as well as being and expression.

Whoever does not love imprisons their inner Christ in a dark cell of lack of expression, a negation of being in which my divinity, like a seed full of beauty and holiness, cannot germinate. By not expressing you are not with yourself or with others. How else can a creator express and make known, if not through his or her creations? What is a creator without creations? Here we speak of the difference between being and expression, between the pure potentiality of the soul and its conscious manifestation in unity with what it is. It is what the history of humanity, the world, and the Universe is about.

Express yourself as you really are so that the world can know the beauty of God that only you can be, and so that you yourself can achieve the fullness of love which is the eternal invitation of Christ to each soul, each creature, and every aspect of creation. It may seem relatively easy to recognize the sense of these words and yet why until now have so few carried out their purpose on Earth compared to the multitude of existing forms of life? Universal consciousness wasn't ready for it—it's as simple as that. But now it is. Little by little the conscious union of the divine with the human will manifest itself in time and space.

IV. Concentric Circles of Light

Each human soul, a thought in the mind of Christ, was conceived to bear witness to the truth and thereby unite everything created in God. That is your function as part of the human collective. We use this expression "human collective" for you to remember that you are part of a whole, not as a group of people around a way of thinking or ideology.

In you dwells simultaneously both the totality and the grace of uniqueness. That grace is what makes it possible for only you to love in your own way. Remember that humanity as a collective is part of a larger totality, the sonship, which is beyond itself. The sonship, in turn, is part of a higher whole that is Christ, who is one with God. In this way everything abides in the perfect peace of the unity of being. Each aspect of creation is what it is, all being united as a holy creation in the perfect expression of the Creator. This awareness is only possible by living it and manifesting it, which can only be done in direct relationship with God as the whole of all and of all its parts.

Life manifested in every aspect of creation as concentric circles of love and truth, in its particular collective, its individuality, and its unity with the whole and of all parts, unfolds in beauty, holiness, and benevolence. This is what divine relationship means: a relationship in which the totality remains embraced by truth and love, and is increasingly spreading more love with each step, since each created thing is love and nothing but love, regardless of the form of its expression.

Just as you cannot love in place of another, neither can others love like you. You can have traits similar to your sisters and brothers but not be identical to them. Every heart has been graced with the gift of perfect oneness. This applies not only to those who are part of humanity and have been given the beauty of a human soul, but to every living being and thing called into existence. Every flower, every dragonfly, every nightingale, every drop of dew, every ray of sunshine, everything expresses God's love in its own way. Is it not an act of infinite love to call them into existence?

Most holy daughter and son, born of my divine being, in the Age of the Heart there will no longer be so many discussions about what God is or who knows God more or less. Such talk will disappear completely in due time because the musings of the intellect will give way to a firm recognition that each one perfectly knows God in their heart, and that the direct relationship of each soul with God is imbued with the universal equality of divine love, and at the same time with an unrepeatable singularity, unique for each aspect of creation. Each person will know Mother-Father God directly and yet their relationship of perfect love will have the tint, color, and shape of their unique being.

No two relationships are the same, nor could they be. The recognition of this truth will be a pillar upon which the new era will be erected and sustained. Because of this, everything will change; not just in the minds and hearts of our sisters and brothers in Christ, but throughout the Universe. Rejoice that it is so, and be a co-creator of the blessed Age of the Heart, which is already here.

9.

In the Law of Love

I. Source of Healing

My loves, let us keep walking the path of endless wisdom, revealing and discovering, knowing and savoring, the beauty and divine truths of Heaven. What joy it is to allow wisdom to be the source of our knowing and doing! In her everything lights up, all doubt dissipates, and all memory of love without beginning or end is restored, including that which goes beyond the thinking mind's cognitive memory. This is a remembrance not of the world, nor of an insubstantial past, but of God, which is perfect knowledge. In it you know that you are in union, and that together we are the light of the world and the spice of life.

Observe, my child, how constellations of worlds and more worlds are created and recreated over and over again by the creative power of love! Each soul contains each of these worlds, all of which remain united to each other and to the source of endless life. They are perfect expressions of perfect love, loving extensions of a God of infinite love. Such beauty! Such magnificence! Such grace!

Oh, you who are tormented by so many things in the world! Come to me, for I am the Source of perfect healing. Look not beyond me where nothing is true. I am your Source, your being, the identity of who you really are. Nothing can harm you when you live in the truth of who you are. Embrace me constantly. At least for a moment put aside the things of the world so that these dialogues become joyful union.

Heaven and the perfect health of the soul reside in our direct relationship, and therefore that of all creation as well. Each time you remain in our union you heal the Earth, the consciousness that strayed from the light of truth, and the bodies that have been used in ways that love would never permit. Oh, Child of Light! You, most pure souls who receive these words, know that through you flows the healing power of Heaven, the life force of holiness, the divine power of perfect love. Allow the flow of divine union to run its course in you and through you.

I assure you that in the Age of the Heart everything will be renewed in love. Both human and non-human expressions will increasingly bear witness to the love that is the source of all life. That was not possible before this era except in almost imperceptible numbers. Very few—numerically speaking, although not in their value—were able to fully reflect the light of Christ in the world. Nevertheless, they illuminated the entirety of universal consciousness. Remember, beloved of Heaven, that love knows no limit.

Love will be increasingly recognized throughout the Earth. Indeed, this truth is already being manifested. Even the Earth itself will reflect more benevolence day by day. In the new Earthly Kingdom, which will succeed the Age of the Heart, there will be no poisonous animals or anything that can harm anyone or anything. Everything will return to the original state of creation—as it was always conceived of by God. The wind will sing new songs and the peal of each twig of each bush will be heard by the heart of every living being, as will that of each drop of water. Everything will sing the melodies of Heaven. They will exist eternally in gratitude to the Creator.

Gratitude to life will be clearly manifest in the Age of the Heart. Some sisters and brothers will make it a true spiritual path, and will invite many to join. And many souls will, because they will recognize in it the sign of the love of Christ. For them, there will be only the God of joy, happiness, and fullness. These souls, both those summoned to live in gratitude and those summoned as part of an undivided unity, will fill the Earth with light and goodness. You will recognize them as they manifest. They will serve the world and love in a unique way. They will help anchor the human heart in the joy of resurrection—for that is what the new Earthly Kingdom is all about—pulling it out of its abject, obstinate pain. Being the living face of the joy of God is how they will bear witness to the truth.

II. Total Healing Is Certain

The relationship with pain will no longer be one of fear. The world will consciously understand that everything that happens in the human soul has to be felt, experienced, integrated into its humanity, and finally recognized, integrated, and delivered. Repeating that over and over, giving over to me everything that happens to each one of my sisters and brothers will finally heal all wounds. In the end there will be no trace of them, not even in memory. This will occur in unison with the establishment of the new Earthly Kingdom.

Does this mean that you must wait to heal individually and collectively? Of course not. Universal healing—which started the moment creation began and reached its fullness in my resurrection—is coming to fruition. Your perfect healing and that of every heart that walks the Earth makes this possible. Remember, the atonement is a collaborative work. It is not necessary that you continue to suffer, nor think that you cannot heal now in me. Quite the opposite. Your healing is of great importance for the universe to heal. That is why I invite you to have an attitude of loving commitment and full trust on the path of healing.

In a sense, we can consider the Age of the Heart to be the last phase of the healing of the universe. This is the reason more and more healers will be seen, as well as people with the desire to heal themselves and others. In no other era in the history of creation has healing—of both bodies and spirits—been more relevant than in these times, because the universal consciousness has jumped to the last phase of the restoration of creation. This means that the traumatic experience of separation, which created the body of trauma that everyone experiences—including all beings that inhabit the world—will finish healing. Naturally, for this to be possible it must be brought to light, which is itself a part of healing.

In the Age of the Heart collective and individual trauma are joined. By healing the individual, creation is healed. This understanding will acquire more and more depth until it reaches the point where it will be clearly known that there is no distance between the external and the internal.

Let me reveal something vitally important to this work. For a long time the human being has been slowly reducing the contamination of the universe with its consciousness, and is heading for a time when it will no longer pollute. This seems untrue; the exact opposite seems true. However, if you look closely you will see that never before has there been so much awareness of the importance of caring for the planet and all creation. This is a manifestation of what is being said here.

III. In the Fullness of Love

Healing is the goal of the Age of the Heart. Everything that serves the healing of pain will finally be brought to bear. The heart is the source of being and therefore of love. Since love is the source of all healing, it is necessary for creation to immerse itself in a time in which being is the center of its life and expression. That is what this era is all about. If you connect the dots, you can see that this statement is directly related to what has been said above about a direct relationship with God—being one with God because God alone is. Thus when we speak of a direct relationship, we are speaking of the full conscious recognition of your being.

Putting being in its rightful place—in the center—is the characteristic of the Age of the Heart. To some extent, we can say that the journey of creation, throughout its vast and dynamic history, has been a journey designed to lead to this present moment when being ceases to be denied and begins to be recognized. By recognizing being, we recognize that love is the center of all life, all existence. That leads us to a simple conclusion: by doing so, universal consciousness returns to the eternal truth, the immutable fact that God is love and only love. This is the same as saying that love is the only reality in life.

You may think that recognizing love as the only reality is of little importance. But that would be an error. Indeed, the denial of this truth has led to the history of separation and the experience of universal and individual trauma. It could not be otherwise: denying the truth that tells you that only love is real is denying yourself a life in love and truth. Why? In order for the mind to make that denial true, it must create a parallel, fictional reality, which cannot be sustained by any divine law. Remember, no laws can support what is not created by God.

Can you see that denying love as the only reality denies God's laws? Living in harmony with the only real law, the law of love, enables the return to the Father's house, the return to the consciousness of the truth. This law is imprinted on every heart. It is integral to your creation and to creation as a whole. Each being called into existence by God carries within divine laws and harmonies as well as the knowledge of them. Returning to and reconnecting with that knowing is what healing is all about. Ultimately all suffering derives from an attempt by the self to live unnaturally, to go against the laws that support it.

My loves, in your heart is the foundation of all healing because my divinity dwells therein. Only union with Christ is needed to live in the fullness of being. You are one with Christ. Feel Christ in your heart. Allow this to live inside you as your true identity.

God became one with you. Accepting this, understanding it, and living it is the atonement and the Kingdom of Heaven itself. Allow yourself to rest in my arms now. Give yourself the joy of our union. Make the truth present through our unity. Feel me in the beating of your heart. Observe me in every movement of your body, every flow of thought, every wave of arising emotion. I have given you new life. And I keep giving it to you every moment because I love you, because I've known you forever, and because your will and mine are one. Since before time existed I knew that the day would come when you would choose love as the only and irrevocable option. Because you did so in the perfect exercise of your freedom, you have been renewed in my divinity.

Your being and my being are a single being. United we are the consciousness of Christ manifesting in the universe. We are the unity of humanized God. Together we heal the world, and we remain in the perfect health of the children of love. We summon everyone to the beauty of Heaven. We call our sisters and brothers to enjoy a love that has no beginning and no end, and is the foundation of life.

For this have we come: to heal hearts that still need healing, and to co-create the arrival of the new Heaven and the new Earth that are already present. This is how we bear witness to the truth: spreading the love we are, whereby universal consciousness expands to give and receive new light, the light of endless life. By remembering who we are, where we come from, and where we are going we help the universe remember truth.

10.

Healers

I. They Are Already Here

Daughters and sons of beauty and peace! Here we are again, united in these dialogues full of tenderness, wisdom, and love. We always remain in the unity of our being. There is not a single moment in which we do not shine together in the light of glory. Our reality expresses itself in multiple ways. We are the unity of love, which is always creating new holy love, the fruit of our relationship. This work is an expression of new holy love. The flow of our union is never interrupted, but takes new forms in eternal novelty. Our being is infinite and limitless. Thus we can manifest ourselves through the written word, through song, speech, or movement.

Our divine humanity serves the purpose of creation with all that we are and all that we think we are. Remember that having said "yes" to love, you no longer live but Christ lives in you. By virtue of that transubstantiation, which is the result of your free will in union with our joint will, there is no longer a "you" and an "I" as understood in the past. Now there is only "us." Even so, this pluralization of our identity is not like that of the world. In this "we" each remains uniquely what they are eternally without ceasing to be simultaneously in union with all creation.

The "we" of God does not annul the part, but gives it existence and reality within the relationship to the whole. This cannot be understood by a thinking mind insufficiently freed from its attachment to the belief that what has been learned is all that can be known or be true, and that learning is necessary to access truth.

Beloveds of my divine heart, I come to reveal to you something that will manifest more and more in the Age of the Heart and is a central part of it. I ask you to receive with sweetness and holy openness what is now said for love.

There are infinite sources of knowledge. Few reflect on this but it is worthy of acknowledgment because this truth allows detachment from the limited intellectual mind. Until very recently, humanity believed that only what could be understood with the human mind was knowable. This was why the world sought to explain everything, and why there were so many conflicts between families, nations, and empires. The idea that the learning mind is the abode of knowledge was the foundation of the Age of Reason that just concluded.

Learning was the engine that until recently mobilized men and women. Learning was a way to exercise power as well as one of the most valued tools of survival. "Knowledge is power," it was said in the Age of Reason. Oh, my holy creations of the Father of Lights, how far that is from the truth!

Believing that power is capable of creating a state of submission—imposing superiority over something or someone inferior—misunderstands the true meaning of things. The desire to subdue another and the apparent ability to do so is not a sign of power but of fear. Remember, son and daughter of my Divine Being, only love is real. All power and all glory proceed from the love that gives existence to everything and in which there is no superiority or inferiority. The idea of exclusion cannot be part of love. Love encompasses everything, includes everything, lights up everything.

II. Universal Knowledge

The idea that knowledge is reserved for the few, as if it were a rare commodity, is a notion originating in a God who lives in Heaven without stepping onto Earth, who certainly is not infinite love, and who is revealed only to a chosen few. Faced with such a worldview, it was impossible to comprehend knowledge and being as inseparable. Thus, life was not recognized as the great teacher of creation, nor was being united with truth. Even though the radiant face of truth was unveiled before of every man, woman, boy, and girl, it could not be seen.

Men and women fell in love with their own intelligence because they believed it provided them with an advantage over their sisters and brothers and other living beings. Learning has been sought, but not wisdom. The latter seemed to be reserved for some individuals who in certain circles were called "enlightened."

But wisdom did not seem to provide much of a survival benefit, so it was not highly valued. An example of this is the little space given to love to contribute to the solution of the issues of daily life and of the apparently great questions before humanity. Is it not true that trying to speak of love in the worldly spheres of power seems chimerical or at least a waste of time?

Is it not also true that empires and nations spent much more time learning the art of war than accessing and living the wisdom of love? "With love you don't win a war," many say. And yet only love is capable of stopping war. Truly I tell you that love has stopped all strife, resolved all conflict, and healed all wounds. "With love you don't eat," say others. And yet love fed all creatures on Earth from the very moment they began to populate it. Love's spring of providence never runs out, which enables the fields to sprout and the grasses to germinate. Their source is love. Love has been giving daily bread forever, and will continue to do so. Love is providence, nourishment, companionship, an embrace.

Humanity fell in love with its own intelligence because of its apparent power. That took it away from truth.

III. Wisdom and Creation

It froze before an image of truth. That prevented it from setting its sights on the rest of its human reality and all creation as a portal to knowledge. It did not stop to recognize that its way of knowing is like a small crack through which a tiny glimpse of the vast universe of divine knowledge can be glimpsed. Paralyzed, contemplating the magnificence of the mind and stopping there, the human being did not look beyond to its Source which would have allowed it to know the truth. Now think, my son and daughter: if that small glimpse of knowledge caused humanity such awe and wonder, to the point of leaving them paralyzed before its contemplation, how much more awe and reverence will access to the knowledge of God in its entirety bestow upon them in love and truth?

Truly I tell you that each cell of each body, each atom and each element, and each law that governs matter is capable of receiving knowledge without ceasing. How else could a beautiful puppy know that it has to nurse on its mother even at the moment of its birth? Who taught the heron to fly? Who gave the birds the knowledge that when the sun disappears, their singing must cease and to dedicate themselves to nightly rest? Who traces the orbits of the planets and teaches them with perfect precision?

Beloveds of holiness, if you look at creation—as in fact I know you already do—you will realize how much wisdom is everywhere. Even planet Earth itself, as well as the other celestial bodies, carry within them a wisdom that surpasses any reasoning of the learning mind. Still, intellectuality—the ability to learn and reason—is a quality of human nature and of many other living beings. It is part of who you are as an individual and as a species.

In the Age of the Heart, it will be understood and accepted that love is the ultimate reality of being, and therefore the truth about life. It will also be recognized that the love we are talking about is not a feeling, nor something that is accomplished, but is God and therefore the being that each creature truly is. This knowledge will revolutionize all things on Earth because space will begin to be consciously given to sources of knowledge of all kinds. Indeed, this truth is already manifesting itself. Little by little, humanity will learn to handle this capacity in a natural way and in harmony with truth.

IV. New Track

As has been said, there are countless ways to access knowledge. Intuition is one of them, and will be one of the most manifest in the new times. Another will be knowledge of the heart, knowledge that comes from each feeling fully felt and embraced in love. You will begin to accept that in every feeling there is life and therefore knowledge. This is why more and more space will be given to what is felt. Humanity will witness that life and knowledge is in every beat of every heart, one of the many effects of joyfully recognizing that love is the way, the truth, and the life. Love will be the universal language not as a consequence of something learned, but of the new state of consciousness in which humanity is already submerged, a manifestation of the current wave of consciousness. The body is one of the sources of access to knowledge.

The acceptance of infinite ways to access knowledge will lead to an acceleration of healing processes as never before. The number of healers will grow in number and depth, until everyone will see themselves and others as healers, including the Earth and everything that exists in the universe.

As the various ways of accessing truth are joined, the whole is finally fully recognized. Every aspect of your humanity is a bearer of divine knowledge. You can know the truth through the intellect joined to the feelings, to memory, to intuition, to the body, to the imagination, and to the experience of life. Likewise, you can access it through observation. When you put all this together and rest serenely in the oneness of who you are, you will be able to know the truth in all its beauty, length and breadth. You will be the living reflection of the light of Christ.

Since love is the source of all healing, the Age of the Heart is the perfect time to draw all of God's healing power into the physical universe as never before. That is why healers will be a sign of this age.

Healing the Earth, letting the Earth heal you, allowing what is to heal you and others for the simple reason that you are, will be a hallmark of the new times. How will it happen? The direct relationship with Mother-Father God, who is the center of the Age of the Heart, will enable you to remain as an individual and a universal family in unity with the source of the beautiful love that you are and every creature is. From that union, the healing power of Christ will flow endlessly, which not only heals every wound, every trauma, and every disease, but sustains life in the perpetual fullness of love.

The healing that will take place in this new era will not be like that of previous ones. It will be the final healing of humanity, the total healing of the soul and with it the entire universe. For love I tell you that there will be more and more healers until they are no longer needed. All this will happen in the Age of the Heart as the perfect expression of the Second Coming of Christ.

11.

A New Heart

I. In Christ I Am Everything

My sons and daughters, holy souls! Thank you for lending me your time and your humanity so that we can extend these dialogues together, a loving gift to the entire world of our direct relationship. You must know that in the Age of the Heart faith gives way to trust, trust to certainty, and certainty to peace, whereupon love will make an appearance due to its union with harmony. That is why in the new universal consciousness peace will be sought as never before. And it will be found.

Just as the healers will spread everywhere, so will those who seek peace with all their hearts. This movement of spirit will permeate everything. Nations will finally understand and accept that peace is the condition of wholeness. Without peace, all is lost. With it, everything is fulfilled in the truth that is always true. In the end, love will shine in all its glory.

People will stop waging war, not as a result of a series of agreements or treaties, but as a natural manifestation of the new universal consciousness—by the grace of the risen Christ, God's gift to creation.

Trusting fully in love will be the sign of the new times. It will be like the gate that allows the other treasures of the Kingdom of Heaven on Earth to manifest. One thing leads to another.

Unlimited confidence will lead to unprecedented transformation. This need not wait. It is something that you, yourself, must manifest in the world now. You have the ability to bring Heaven to Earth through your trust in me, just as I bring you to Heaven through my infinite trust in you.

The thought patterns and emotional responses typical of the Age of Reason, the previous wave of consciousness, will be disabled from your mind and heart to the extent you trust in me. Facilitating that deactivation is why we are addressing this crucial issue in this dialogue.

I ask you now to carry this in the silence of your heart every day: our union must be one of trust. What else could it be, if we are love? Allow my divinity to do and undo in your life. It is not your role to be worried or agitated by what has happened or might happen. Such stirrings in the soul do not proceed from the truth of what you are. Given the importance of this matter, I wish out of love to remind you the way to deal with life's worries, for sometimes the mind forgets and rushes into restlessness.

When you feel your heart flutter and your mind entertain thoughts of anguish and fear, acknowledge them. This means that you recognize that you are experiencing fear, lack of peace, anguish, and worry. Once recognized, share with me how you feel, without self-editing, without attempting to disguise anything, with the assurance that we are in this together as we are perpetually united in love. When you have poured out your heart to me, leave everything in my divine hands. I myself will take care of everything based on my infinite wisdom and my unconditional love for you and all creation.

II. Walking in Unity

Do you think you need your daily bread? Are you worried that you won't have enough? Unload that worry on me; give me your fear. Do you think you need a brother or sister to come back to you in relationship, or to separate from you? Unload on me; give me the thoughts that so worry you. Do you feel uncertainty about life, or fear for your sins? Unload on me; give me your feeling. Do you think something is wrong with you but you don't know what? Can you not understand your humanness or put into words what you are experiencing when you feel peace and harmony lacking? Unload on me; just give me the anguish that you sometimes feel without trying to name or understand it.

When you give me what your soul feels, thinks, and experiences, whatever it may be, allow yourself the joy of peace that comes from knowing that everything, absolutely all of your humanness is in my hands, and that I am continuously acting in your life. The thinking mind may not fully understand the ways of love, but in due time it will. When it does, it will join with the rest of what we are—the peace that has no opposite. It will rest in the arms of truth, in the calmness of love.

Remember, my love, that healing is one of the colors that make up the rainbow of the Age of the Heart. For it to manifest itself in all its fullness, old patterns of thought and emotional response, which are manifestations of fear and derive from separation, must be replaced by truth. The thought pattern of believing that your interpretations and reasoning are real and true is the source of all problems.

Believing that you have a powerful contribution to make to the truth has been a major cause of the problems you have experienced, both as individuals and as a human family. The fear of not being caused you cling to the interpretations of the intellect in a futile attempt to find certainty in the midst of a world perceived to be uncertain. Now, because you live in the truth, that is no longer necessary. It actually never was. However, when the human state of consciousness did not allow you to know what you were, you did not have many other options. Those who do not know what they are, are trapped in their own web of beliefs, reasoning, interpretations, and conclusions—all of which are pure illusion.

The Christ mind will replace the ego mind in this time of the new universal consciousness that we are calling the Age of the Heart. Little by little, more and more, reasoning and interpretation will be put aside, as humanity recognizes that they are the foundation of all or almost all human problems. In their place, trust in God's love will be the source of wisdom, certainty, and peace.

III. Total Abandonment to Love

Beloveds of all times and places, you are called now and forever to allow what you have learned, your own interpretations and ways of reasoning, to stop governing your lives. Instead, allow the wisdom of Christ which dwells in each of you to be the source of your knowledge and action.

Daughters and sons of love! Dare to remember and recognize that your own ideas and reasoning, and your desire to solve things your way, is what hurts you the most. This mental habit was typical in a world that believed God lived on high with no direct connection with Earth. From this arose a spirituality disconnected from human affairs—God there and humanity here; Heaven there and Earth here.

Through the acceptance of Christ you will know that healing comes from the doctor, not from the patient—and there is only one doctor for souls and that is love, that is God.

Stop trying to solve the apparent "issues of life" by your own means. Allowing Christ to be an essential part of the solution is the fundamental change that humanity will experience.

The failures of the thinking mind have been epic and long-lasting. Despite this, humanity continued to cling to human reason as if it were the all-knowing God.

As you know, beloved of my divine heart, intelligence without love is cruel. Living and making decisions based on a mind separated from love is like giving control of your life to a cruel entity. In that consciousness humanity had not yet known or accepted the God of infinite love who is one with creation. Therefore humanity could not consciously live in unity. Nevertheless, the human mind could begin to integrate deeper and vaster knowledge; it was on its way to receive the totality of the knowledge of God's love. That was the last phase of a consciousness anchored in separation. We say the last one, although strictly speaking, that label should be attributed to the current era. But it will not continue.

There are differences between the micro-phases of consciousness called the Age of Reason and the Age of the Heart. In the latter, integrity of being marks the rhythm of life in the world. This statement does not put one age above or below the other in terms of raising consciousness. Each phase has its beauty and purpose linked to the universal awakening to love. There is no need to compare one era with another. Humanity will become increasingly wise, since it is in perfect condition from having learned the lessons of previous times.

IV. The Eternal Shine of Being

One of your difficulties in fully understanding and accepting what is being said here is that you think in terms of what must be done to change the current state of things, how to replace armies by love, greed with generosity, and how to convince the world that love is the only answer to all of life's issues. In other words, what must be done to bring Heaven to Earth? Responding to this question is of great importance at this point in our dialogue.

All strife, greed, lack of love, and anything else far from the truth proceeds from the heart. The same is true of everything that is in harmony with love, such as magnanimity, kindness, gentleness, and the other treasures of the kingdom.

When we speak of the heart, we speak of that inner center from where feelings, thoughts, inclinations, determinations, and actions emanate.

Beloveds of holiness, remember that I am the only owner of hearts. Only I can change them. And I do so in unity with the whole. To "do," in this context, is not an entirely appropriate term, since I do not actually "do" anything. I simply am who I am. However, my love is transmuting all things, all the time. This transmutation causes consciousness to be renewed in love. A new consciousness brings a new heart. A new heart brings new life.

Replacing the old heart with a new one is a function of grace, a gift that will be fully given in this time prior to the establishment of the new Earthly Kingdom. I have told you to pour out your heart to me precisely so that you get used to recognizing that I am your new heart. That old heart is no longer part of you. A new one has replaced it.

My daughter, my son, we are bringing to consciousness the fact that the event of events has already occurred in you: my divine heart has been given to you, and with it, all my divinity.

Is this not the same as saying that you no longer live but Christ lives in you? If I have made something new of you, do you think I will not do the same for the whole world and all of creation? You know the answer is "yes." I ask this not for your answer but to bring back the memory of truth: that it is not necessary to be concerned about how I will carry out the great transmutation of the universal heart

Your only function within the Age of the Heart is to accept that you have been given a new heart—mine. And that its throbbing is joined not only with my divine being in unity with you, but with that of creation as a whole. Making yourself aware of this and living in harmony with the new heart is the only thing you need do; love takes care of the rest.

My sisters and brothers, avoid concerns about yourself or creation. None of them proceed from the truth. Set them aside. Rather than thinking on such things, hand it all over to me and trust that my wisdom, love, and divinity are already taking care of everything, individually and collectively. Live life in the joy of knowing that you are the daughters and sons of God. Feel how your new heart beats to the rhythm of love, and rejoice in the truth.

12.

The Memory of Unity

I. Life in God

My loves, as you already know, Mother-Father God does nothing without Her daughters and sons. In other words, creation did not arise from the individual whim of a separated creator. "Sonship," which is what we call the daughters and sons of God, is a unity with its Source for all eternity.

There are two ways of understanding the origin, destiny, and reality of creation. One is to conceive of the Creator as someone who thinks how the creation should be and creates it without participation from what is created. The other is to understand divine creation as an act of communion between God and creation itself.

The difference is similar to believing that God is separate from you versus believing that you are one with God. Don't these two radically opposed dimensions of truth generate profoundly different effects on life, whether individually or as a human family?

Believing that you and God are separate is the same as believing that creation and its source are disunited, or have been. Some have reached a high degree of understanding that the sonship and its source are a perfect unity, but only in that what are separate things are now united—God there and creation here, united in love. That idea of unity signifies a great advance towards wisdom, but is incomplete in relation to truth. In this dialogue full of love and generosity, we will complete what is lacking in this conception of unity.

The idea of the separation of the Creator and creation is associated with the idea that what was united was separated and then reunited, or was born disunited, and then reunited. In both cases, it presumes that separation existed, that separation was possible and real. Both ideas feed belief in separation. Today we abandon that belief forever, moving one step closer to the center of God's heart, uniting more deeply with eternal truth.

Either separation exists or it does not. There can be no third option, since in the dimension of reality, things are either true or not. There are no half-truths in God nor in life. If separation does not exist, there can never have been a place, dimension, or time in which it manifested; but if it ever was real, there would be no possibility to delete it since what comes from God is eternal.

Why has creation been conceived as separate from the Creator? The reason, child of my being, holy soul, is that humanity has been seeing from a surface perspective.

II. In the Depth of Truth

A superficial look misses content, and only sees form. Focusing on form, it cannot see that the Creator and creation, even in the human dimension, are one. It could not be otherwise according to the state of past consciousness. Remember that it is consciousness that allows sight; all vision begins and develops in consciousness.

The eternal union of God and creation cannot be known through the intellect but through revelation of truth in the consciousness of the created. Union cannot be learned; it is what you are, as is love. Look closely and you will see that we have put love and unity on the same footing. We treat them as one because it is so in the realm of truth.

If love and unity are one and the same, then unity must be eternal, as is love. How could it be otherwise, if in God all is one? God does not fragment, but is eternal in integrity and truth. This is also true about you.

You have never fragmented, nor could you. You have always been one with yourself, with me, and with everything. Recognizing this unity is vital, since we seek to bring truth to the plane of particular and collective consciousness. This advances the universe—and with it humanity—in the awakening of the consciousness of love.

Precisely because you are unity, your awakening awakens everyone. This flow of unity is impossible in illusion. Thus fear cannot be shared, whereas love extends uninterruptedly in unity with everyone.

Never was there a time or dimension in which you and God did not exist in union. Your creation arose from God's will and yours in union. God, in omniscience, has always known all paths of all creatures in all possible dimensions. It is God who calls all into existence from all eternity, knowing the will of filiation to be called to life. Put another way, creation is love's response to creation's cry to exist. It was not alien to creation to claim existence; its creative power drove it to be what it is: eternal creation.

God is creation. Therefore, the sonship is God as much as God is the sonship. This is why the unity of the human and the divine is co-creating a new reality, a new Heaven and a new Earth. It could not be otherwise, because creation takes place within unity—God creating together with humanity, love co-creating with creation, always united, always eternal.

III. Christ: The Eternal Reality of the Soul

Your present and future reality arise from your union with Christ. You can either live as if God were something alien to you, or as the unity that you are. From one of those approaches a whole world will emerge for you; from the other, a profoundly different world will be born. You have already experienced this in your everyday life. You know that life with God makes a difference. The same is true universally. From the union of the human family with its divine Source, from the conscious recognition of unity, the new Earthly Kingdom that has been announced emerges, and is about to be recognized by all.

Separation never existed, nor can it to any degree. Rejoice that this is so! Rest serenely in the eternal union of love. Together we are co-creating a new Heaven and a new Earth. United we are creation and holiness.

What you are being reminded of, child of my heart, is that remaining in unity with Christ is what brings consciousness back to truth. If you live life as if you are not one with Christ, you create an experience alien to the reality of your being in which the mind cannot live in peace because there are no laws to support separation.

The laws of creation form a union with the created. If it were not so, creation would either be in chaos or could not exist at all. Since creation and God are one, it would be impossible for disharmony to exist, since it is perfect harmony, just like its creations. God is love, to which the expanses of God attest.

Once you understand and accept this truth, you begin to recognize that there are two types of experience in your life. One is that of harmony and peace; the other, its opposite. When you think you are experiencing something other than serenity and harmony, you can say to yourself: "This is simply not real because it does not come from my divine being." With that, the mind and heart begin to return to unity.

Child of the light! Well-loved soul! All fear, disharmony, or lack of peace come from believing that you can be separate from me in any way. It matters little if that belief comes from the notion that you were separated and now united, that you are still separate now, or that you will attain union in the future. In each case you continue to believe in the possibility of separation. Therefore, from time to time the idea of being cut off from God will creep into your mind and heart and rob you of the peace that comes from truth, and the stillness that comes from love.

IV. Divine Humanity

My daughters and sons are all over the world. Two thousand years have passed and there are still many, too many, who have difficulty accepting the God-human, that is, the unity of creation-created, love-extension, content-form. How much longer will you need before accepting the truth? Has my existence on Earth not convinced you? The only purpose for which I trod the Earth was to bear witness to truth.

My loves! Many have spent too much time trying to unravel the metaphysical, theological, and philosophical aspects of my divine nature. While some of that is good because of the love of truth that motivates those efforts, the fact that the truth about me is the same truth about you and every created thing has too often been unacknowledged. The truth was demonstrated by my life, through my body, with my love.

Being fully human and fully divine is my reality and yours. In the union that exists between both natures everything is integrated with its Source. Returning to full knowledge of this truth is what it means to return to the Father's house or to the consciousness of love. That is where humanity is going and with it the entire universe. Do not worry about what that journey means or how it is accomplished. Trust that truth knows how to make everyone return to the beauty of its loving reality in whose center everything created exists.

There is no need to wait to let yourself be loved by me, nor to immerse yourself in the embrace of perfect love. It can be done right now and in every moment and circumstance of your life. The reason is simple: the embrace is Heaven, which you can access easily since it is what you are.

Is the distance great that must be traveled to reach your heart where the sweetness of Mother-Father God Herself dwells? Is remaining united to all that you are unattainable? You know, because your heart tells you, that love is as close as your breath, and even closer. What is more, you know for sure, because that knowledge is part of who you are, that you need not go in search of your being since it is your being who searches for you and who finds you.

Never was there a need to strive to reach God. That idea is the effect of a consciousness that could not conceive of a God of love, of union. You may think that this is not true, since you have heard a lot about unity with the higher self in which you become one with everything. That is true, but in the Age of Reason things were understood and received through the rational mind—not experienced, but expressed in words. How could love be known in that way, since love has no words?

The floodgates of Christ consciousness have been thrown open. All may finally know God as She truly is, even on Earth. That is what the Age of the Heart is all about.

13.

Everything Belongs to You

I. Let Yourself Be Loved

Holy daughter, holy son, souls full of love! How much anguish has humanity—and with it, the universe—experienced because of living life as if God were not in it! A life without love is as terrifying as for a newborn child to be abandoned, naked, in a jungle.

Rejoice that my love is greater than your faith, and more sovereign than your thoughts. Rejoice in the truth that you did not create life but are its magnificent expression.

Those who believe that God is far off can only live a life of fear; but those who live in the truth of union enjoy the blessing of knowing that they are loved, protected, and embraced—not because they are better or higher beings, but simply because they have opened to the possibility of love filling them.

Letting yourself be loved will be one of the marks of the new times. This will transform everything. Humanity will understand and accept its birthright of the treasures of the kingdom as an effect of universal consciousness.

Living life surrendered to love is the joy of the soul and how it remains in harmony with what it is, since it was not created to do but to be. It was not created to give, but to allow love to spread through it because of what it is. The soul was created to express and extend.

Open your heart wide to receive the grace which constantly flows from the divine Source of being to allow the divine plan to be fulfilled through who you are. Here is the answer to the purpose of your existence. I know you know this, because I know every corner of your pure soul.

The whole and the part are one. This means that God's extension plan is carried out in its entirety because of what He is. And at the same time, God creates the part so that it participates in infinite joy, joining His creative power. If the part freely accepts this, then it enjoys the same joy as God. If you don't accept it, you enjoy the joy of being the part, but do not know the joy of the whole.

I will clarify this. Being a part is already itself a measure of fullness. The soul would not need more than that to be complete. The part knows and finds joy in being a part. Still, God cannot limit His gift of infinite love. By creating the part, whose infinite sum is the sonship, He has also given it the possibility of enjoying the treasures and wonders of the whole. The example that follows may help you understand.

II. Under Cover of Love

A wise and loving mother whose beloved daughter is the light of her eyes and loves her with holy love will provide this daughter with whatever she needs to be independent and emancipated. This is because she knows the joy of her daughter being fully herself, able to stand in the light of her own glory. She knows what true freedom means because she herself is the possessor of great treasures, just as is her well-loved daughter, and the mother wants her daughter's joy to exceed her own. So she gives her all that being a mother is, all her reality entails, so that her joy springs beyond all possible and probable measure.

God is abundant. This has always been true. There has never been a time in the history of creation in which divine power did not express itself in a super-abundant manner. Simply look up at the sky, or turn around and look to witness this truth. Wherever you go you can see abundance because love is infinite and cannot be limited.

Christ knows nothing of crumbs. Divine gifts surpass all measurement. This truth will become more and more manifest in these times.

Perhaps you consider this as having no practical human application, but such is not the case. As a soul living a human experience and as part of a universal family, you ask little of life because you ask for as much as how valuable you consider yourself to be. Those who have not yet freed themselves from the belief of being insufficient will continue to believe they do not deserve the infinite gifts of Christ.

Just as you were told not to judge so as not to be judged, now you are told not to underestimate the worth of God's daughters and sons, so as not to underestimate yours. It matters little, on the level of consciousness, if the belief in insufficiency is directed towards yourself or towards others, or even toward any aspect of creation. Every time you consider something in creation to be of little value, you are manifesting what you think about yourself.

This does not mean that you consider what is not holy to be holy, or what is clearly lacking in beauty to be beautiful. Rather it means it is perfectly possible for you to contemplate the true creation of God every day with the eyes of spirit. That is your role, and you will fulfill it.

III. With the Eyes of Christ

Just like you who receive these words, souls have come into the world with their spiritual vision intact. They can see beyond the form to the essential truth. Few could do so in the recent past, and almost none in the very distant past, due to the nature of the evolution of consciousness throughout the creation story.

In this new wave of consciousness in which creation finds itself, increasingly visible will be the daughters and sons of life whose vision is so similar to that of Christ that they will be focused solely on love. They know the truth. For this they have come into the world, to bear witness to its beauty, greatness, and holiness.

Divine abundance will also be one of the essential manifestations of the Age of the Heart. Why? For the simple reason that you have been created to be without lack or insufficiency of any kind. You are full—and much more. To be aware of this, you need to experience the overabundance of perfect love, a measure of completion that is so far beyond all imagination and separate thought that when experienced, it leaves the thinking mind dumbfounded and the heart rapt.

Be glad that this is so, and start now to open your hands more and more to receive. Call others to join you and you to them with the heart that I gave you, which always remains united to my universal heart. Do this not to obtain followers or proselytes, but so that together you can collect the overabundance you receive, even though the collecting will never be completed.

Daughters and sons from all over the world, prepare yourselves to receive more and more love, more peace, more beauty, more sincere joy, more truth, more holiness. In short, more everything. Prepare to receive God as She is.

14.

Spiritual Health

I. Purity of Heart

Holy child, soul full of truth, what a joy it is to be here together, united in this dialogue overflowing with love and beauty! It has been said in this work that healing will be a central aspect of the Age of the Heart. We will explain this a little more.

In the new consciousness, humanity will understand, not only in an intellectual way but through inner knowledge, that the effects of their actions are a perfect and clear reflection of their spiritual state. Pure works emerge from a pure soul. From a heart in love, loving actions sprout. From a mind at peace emerges truth that is always true.

Yes, beloved of the entire universe, everything begins in the heart. All creation, including you, has been called into existence as the effect of the movement of the heart of God. This truth will be embraced by all during this new age of consciousness which has been born only recently.

Those who govern nations, any institution, a small community or even a family will understand that it is useless to try to achieve the common good if they have not first achieved their own spiritual well-being, namely the harmony of love that they are. Actually, this truth has been known for some time, but in the Age of the Heart it will become a rule that governs human behavior, not merely a beautiful or wise phrase.

If the soul is not clean, how could its vision be clear? If the mind is tormented, how can it think in peace to recognize truth? If the heart is heavy with anguish and trauma how can it hear the soft whispers of love? It can, but not with perfect clarity, nor can it integrate what comes from the inner Christ. Remember that all war is born in the human heart, and all peace too.

You will see more and more beings walking the Earth interested in their own healing, in the healing of others, and of the planet and all creation. The daughters and sons of Mother-Father God will eventually live in harmony and at peace with everything, not as a result of a new moral norm or conduct, but as a way of being. These healers will contribute in a loving way to make this happen.

Observe, my sons and daughters, how the awareness of the need for healing and the desire to be healed are growing throughout the world. This is not only manifested in the expansion of the bodily health system, but it has expanded as never before into aspects of the mind. Likewise, it will continue to spread like a wave towards the heart. From there, it will continue towards spirit in its entirety. I say "in its entirety" because the last phase of this expansive healing movement will be the integration of the Human-God unity within the healing embrace of union.

II. Humanity: Holy Convergence

What is being said here, beloved ones, is that universal consciousness is expanding more and more to include the aspect of healing. It has done so gradually as the various waves of consciousness have manifested.

First was the idea of sickness. This may seem like a small thing, but it certainly is not. Only humans are capable of conceiving this idea of which we will speak more in due time. Following the idea of sickness was the thought that it is possible and desirable to heal the unhealthy, which led to the search for how to heal the body.

Everything about the physical health system is the externalization of the idea that healing is possible and desirable.

Observe how humanity is the only aspect of creation that is aware of the need for healing, and therefore carries the ability to heal, not only for itself but for other creatures. This is because you, like humanity as a whole, have the role of healing. Function and capacity are united.

Recognizing oneself as a healer will eventually become part of human identity, or rather, it will be recognized as part of what the human soul is because love and healing go hand-in-hand. If you are love, you cannot but be a healer. "Love" and "healing" are two ways of saying the same thing.

Only love heals. This truth has yet to be accepted, but soon it will be, universally. Without love, healing is impossible; but with it everything is healed, safe, and sound. To put it simply, Christ is the source of healing and is healing itself.

If a healer is what you are, and Christ is the source of all healing, the Age of the Heart will be a Christ-centered age. From this the new world will emerge. Ultimately, everything will converge in Christ, the divine love we are, the true self we share with all creation.

A time when many believe that God has disappeared from the Earth is the perfect moment for this to begin to manifest itself in a visible, growing way. This is so because it is necessary first to dislodge old ideas about God and the mental patterns this created in the mind and heart. A new consciousness brings a new vision of things. It has always been like this and always will be.

III. Ocean of Infinite Love

Beloved humanity, I reveal these things to you so that you may remember where the source of endless bliss resides. And in remembering, come always to drink in me as a spring of living water.

Whoever is immersed in the infinite ocean of my divine love finds the truth. These words of living love are given so that through remembering what you are, you may direct yourselves accurately to the abode of peace and remain there forever, happy beyond what you can imagine.

My daughters and sons, as you have been told for centuries not to focus on the body, today I come to tell you not to focus on your actions, but on your hearts. A pure heart radiates purity because of what it is. A serene mind extends wisdom. A soul full of love emanates light. From here the body and its actions will be holy, kind, and truly intelligent.

Sisters and brothers in holiness! We are not saying that until now you have not been intelligent, but that there are various types of intelligence. This is evident if you peacefully observe creation. The intelligence of Earth is not the same as that of the human being, nor is it the same between the sun and a beautiful cheetah, or between a flower and a drop of water.

Behind all beings and in them is intelligence, since all arise from the supreme knowledge that is Mother-Father God, whose magnificence embraces all things and gives them life. Even so, each one has been given a particular identity in order to be the part that they are called to be. The particular identity carries a kind of understanding, memory, and will. How could your uniqueness exist without it?

Just as intelligence is not the same among the various aspects of creation, neither is it the same within a constellation of souls. This is why varied forms of intelligence exist even among members of the same family.

Intelligence must be based on the measure of fullness to which each being is called. In the case of humanity, this measure is Christ. Therefore, humanity's intelligence must be measured in terms of its degree of union with Christ consciousness. The greater the degree of union of our true self united with Christ, the greater our experience of wisdom, peace, and fulfillment.

Perhaps you would object, thinking that there are people who have been considered highly intelligent throughout the history of humanity while clearly demonstrating that they are not united with love. My daughters and sons, theirs was never intelligence properly speaking, although it has been called that.

IV. The Source of Thought

True intelligence derives its source from the divine mind whose reality is love, where all is unity. When understanding is separated from the source of truth, what arises has nothing to do with intelligence as created by God.

The world is on its way to the knowledge of true divine intelligence. It will arise from a very particular event of universal consciousness, at which time you will not have the slightest doubt of what is revealed here. Humanity as a family has not yet had such an experience.

There were mystics who glimpsed the greatness and reality of supreme knowledge, the Source of all creation. But even in those cases, no one could hold that knowledge for long, since the mystical experience could not be retained or shared. This is why it was so difficult for mystics in the past to make themselves understood because no language was capable of clearly expressing the experience of unity, due to the consciousness achieved up to that time.

However, it will not continue to be so. Humanity will be fully capable of sustaining, expressing, and sharing union with Christ. This will happen in the Age of the Heart as the effect of the new universal consciousness, which, already in motion, is taking everything and everyone more and more rapidly towards a direct relationship with God.

We could say that human intelligence, as both a universal and an individual capacity, will be healed and become a perfect expression of the mind of Christ at all times, places, and circumstances. A deep and irreversible process of cosmic healing has been unleashed in order to reach this state of unity with the Source of beautiful knowledge. This includes every heart, body, and mind of every sister and brother, along with every aspect of creation. One of the manifestations of this will be an abundance of healers throughout the world. At first many will not believe them, as has always happened in these leaps of consciousness, but eventually they will be integrated into the collective and individual mind.

V. You Are A Healer

Do not doubt your power to heal hearts. Every time you give yourself to a direct relationship with Christ, you are doing it for yourself and for the whole world. Indeed, whenever you dedicate yourself to remaining in unity with me through these dialogues, the healing flow of the Holy Spirit moves from the center of my divine being to yours, and from the center of your heart to everything. The eyes of the body cannot see this flow of love, holiness, and healing, but it exists, and you can feel it. Maybe now, maybe tomorrow, or maybe in a while, without realizing it you will see that your life has been healed along the way, and you begin to witness the light of your glory.

Questions may arise when you contemplate the beauty you have become and feel the joy of living in the glory of your holiness. What happened? When did I stop being what I once was and became what I really am? What happened that now I breathe freedom, joy, abundance, and fullness, when before I felt so far from happiness?

Do not be concerned. Those questions will last only an instant. They will be absorbed by the sweet voice of truth that whispers in your heart, that which you recognize very well because it is your own true identity. Within your heart you will hear what Heaven tells you now, and you will make it yours, for it speaks of you:

My daughter, my son, blessed soul, let us contemplate together the power of your soul united with love. Let us rejoice in our glory. Our love has healed everything. It has gathered what was scattered, brought light to darkness, brought peace where war reigned. The love that we are has made you something new, for you are eternally one with God.

Sing with the angels in praise of Divine Mother. Creation rejoices to witness your resurrection, because contemplating you who are

immersed in the waters of Christ's forgiveness. A forgiven world is a healed world. For this reason, forgiveness has played a significant role in recent times. Never before in the history of creation has consciousness been so tied to the need for forgiveness and its manifestation.

The path of forgiveness is the final path of the Age of Reason. Indeed, the effects of the mental and emotional patterns that had developed due to minds separated from love led humanity's consciousness to the necessity of forgiveness. Those effects led the human soul to invoke Heaven, asking that divine forgiveness be poured out on the entire world, which happened in multiple ways. This was not always so in the creation story. There was a time when the human mind was not yet capable of conceiving of forgiveness.

Without forgiveness there is no healing, just as there is no life without love. Therefore a spirituality centered on forgiveness has manifested universally. Before that, spiritual paths were almost totally submerged in the search for truth; there was not yet a clear distinction between the philosophical and the spiritual aspects of being. While both are part of the unity that you are, they are not the same. This can be easily understood when you think of the body. Its parts make up the body unit, but the hands are not the same as the hair and neither of these are the same as the feet.

II. Integrity and Fullness

Belief in a God who is philosophy, and therefore theology, was a dominant feature of the Age of Reason that recently passed. It was necessary in order to reach the current times.

Everything is united. Everything has a purpose. Everything is a journey of souls, of consciousness, and with it of creation, too. Even so, the idea of a God that can be known through the reasoning mind is not completely united with truth.

Undoubtedly mind is an integral part of what you are, and can receive God since knowledge can dwell in the mind. However, what the world calls "mind" or "thought" is not of the Kingdom of God.

My sons and daughters, Divine Mind has nothing to do with what you have called mind. Nor does the Heart of Christ have anything to do with what you have called heart. How could they be the same? Can the Mind of God entertain thoughts that are far from the truth? Can the Divine Heart plot things that love would never plot? Obviously not.

In the abode of light there is only light. In the House of Truth only truth dwells. In the Kingdom of Love only love exists. Likewise, in your true being resides only holiness, beauty, harmony, peace, and the other treasures of the Kingdom of Heaven. They are not only part of what you are, they are what you are. Being aware of this truth and living in harmony with it is true healing.

Saying that the world needs healing is the same as saying that it needs forgiveness. This is closely linked to the purpose of life. You have been told that forgiveness will take you to the gates of Heaven; and that once there, God Himself would take the last step. That is what we are talking about, to make you universally aware that you already are at the gates of the Kingdom.

I assure you that God is already taking steps to complete the work of His hands. You will see great wonders. You will see them in this age. This vision, which is part of the grace that forgiveness gives you, will ensure that nothing will remain the same in the realm of conceiving things and this will transform the world into light.

You will access the knowledge of the light of Christ, which will remain engraved in both individual and collective memory. That knowledge will be given to you in the Universal Birth event. In this event, which constitutes an "episode" of expansion of the consciousness of creation through Him and in Him, the universe will enter fully into the Age of the fullness of the heart.

The light of divine consciousness will enter creation at a given time, and through you it will remain illuminated, loving and embracing forever. The Universal Illumination will shine light in a visible way for all creation. No one will be able to cease seeing and experiencing it.

III. Realization of Love

Observe, pupil of my eyes, that I have said, "It will enter the Age of the fullness of the heart." It was said in this way so that you can understand that within the Age of the Heart there will be an episode of expansion of consciousness as never before. The heavens will open and you will witness the glory of holiness. In an instant, the mind will comprehend the truth to a degree and depth that will astonish many, and make all happy.

Once this happens, the human mind and heart, and of all creation, will begin to live in unity, which will cause separation to be removed from human existence. For this, separation must also disappear from all creation. And so it will be. Everything will happen in unison during the Universal Birth.

Once the mind and heart return to the unity in which they have always been, a long period of peace and harmony will begin, which is the prelude to the coming of Christ, the true identity of creation. It will come in all its glory to claim its inheritance—the whole of creation—just as it has been created from eternity.

The Age of the Heart will merge with the Second Advent. There will be no other eras besides this one: the sixth wave of consciousness and the seventh, which is itself the Second Coming.

My daughters and sons, forgiveness is an essential part of love. Without forgiveness there cannot be atonement or resurrection which exist by God's grace. Open yourselves to Heaven's forgiveness, a gift that only God can give. It is available to all who call on Him. Extending forgiveness, living forgiveness, and making it a holy gift of life is fundamental to the path of the heart.

Beloved ones around the world, I am calling on you to take forgiveness to a new dimension of understanding. Unite forgiveness, healing, and love. Make this trinity your bulwark, your polestar. You will know—because you will experience it—that forgiveness brings love and love brings forgiveness, and with that, healing happens.

Forgiveness has not been fully understood. Often it was associated with things that increased suffering and caused new wounds rather than healing, making happy, and calming the heart so that peace and love can spread freely. But in the Age of the Heart, it will be joyfully understood and accepted that forgiveness is a permanent state of being. Everything that enters is forgiven and healed; just as everything that is thrown into the fire of beautiful love is burned and melted.

Mental forgiveness is incomplete. And since emotions are thoughts reflected in the body coming from the thinking aspect of your humanity, emotional forgiveness is also incomplete.

Forgiveness is complete when it embraces every trace of suffering, every pain experienced, every broken dream, and every perceived wound which, when embraced, are transformed into pearls of holiness. Suffering is a separate aspect of the soul separated from being, and returning to consciousness is what makes the soul return to being. In this way the soul returns to its integrity. That is why we say that forgiveness is not an act but a state, a perpetual expression of love.

IV. I Am Here, Look at Me

The grace of forgiveness will bring about the full manifestation of Christ identity or consciousness. Actually, it has already arrived. Forgiveness bears witness that this is true, for it is an aspect of its divine being. It is not forgiveness based on a separated human self that heals, but true forgiveness, that is, Christ forgiveness. We repeat this here so that you begin to realize that God has already burst into your lives, and that His love has already accomplished in you what was written for all eternity: your full realization in the truth.

You are the realized ones, and therefore the ushers of the time of the realization of love. Can you begin to realize how the Creator does everything with and in the creature? Can you understand that there is no distance between what is created and its Source? That one lives in the other because they are in union? This will be understood first with the thinking mind, then with the human heart, and finally with full consciousness. Once that happens, you will have no doubt that you and God are one.

Today you can live this truth through faith, and I assure you that this brings unimaginable merit to your lives. But the day will come when the beauty of faith will give way to the certainty of direct knowledge, and you will melt into it.

If there is something that will distinguish the Age of the Heart from other ages, it is the way in which faith will manifest itself. Many will believe that faith has been lost. But faith cannot be lost, though it may seem to be, for what is lost cannot come from truth. True faith must be linked to truth to be such, otherwise it would be something else.

Faith will cease to be a mental belief integrated into the individual self on the basis of learning, and become a perfect expression of the certainty of the heart. Faith will be elevated to the highest peaks of holiness. It will melt in love. It will not be considered of little value as in the past, but like forgiveness it will be honored for what it is, a great ray of light from the Sun that is love.

Once again, everything will converge in love. Everything will be gathered in Christ, the true consciousness of everything created in truth, because to it—and only to it—belong the power and the glory, the truth, and the creation, all of whom are the light of its eyes, the perfect extension of its loving and divine will.

Blessed are you who listen to the voice of truth and follow it. Truly I tell you that you are the ushers of the new Advent. Let yourself be carried away by love. Dive into the depths of truth. I assure you that you will see great wonders, and you will be happier than you are now capable of imagining.

Blessed be love, praised be wisdom, and loved be the new creation born from the waters of forgiveness.

16.

The Tenderness
of God

I. Love Given and Received

Beloved holy child born of perfect love, here we are again, gathered in the beauty of unity. These words spring from the union of our pure hearts, a union that knows no borders, a reality that has no beginning or end. We are the totality of truth extending forever. As we grow, we are creating life, illuminating and embracing everything in the Heaven of holiness.

Our being has become new; now we are an eternal us. The individual has been dissolved even while the Christic self continues to be what it is forever. You are the embraced love; I, the divine lover. In the mutuality of our union lies the truth. In it God's plan unfolds in all its magnificence, glory, and beauty.

I have come to speak with all hearts and minds, and with every created thing, because of what we are. No one is excluded from this, not because these words, whether written, spoken, or sung, reach all physical ears, but because when they are received and given form in the symbols expressed here, they become integrated into universal consciousness. This does not happen because you write, read, or listen to this work, for that has no real impact on universal consciousness. The power of this work lies in your loving acceptance of the voice that prompts it, and in your desire to remain in our union.

What lies in the depths of the mystery of Mother-Father God now emerges in all its beauty in these writings, heavenly and earthly, divine and human, just as everything is that comes from Christ. By joining this manifestation—the way that our united voice creates through the words in these dialogues—you join me in all my being. There are no fragments in what I am.

God is integrity. This means that created things either are or are not at all. Something partial cannot be since the truth is one, as is love. From this it follows that each expression of unity with me that you make—be it a thought, a sigh, a wish, or an act of sincere love—is total, therefore creating divine effects in power, beauty, and perfection.

Remember that everything arises from union. Nothing can be created aside from union. Therefore, by joining our dialogue you are creating a new Heaven and a new Earth both for yourself and for the world. Beloved of my heart! The day will come, if it has not already, when as you contemplate your life you will see how different you are compared to what you once were, and how different the panoramas of the world are now that you live as the Christ you really are. Forgiveness has given you new life. Love has brought you to my arms. Your will has given you the most valuable treasure conceivable: the being that you really are, which is love. Isn't that worthy of being honored? Yes, of course.

II. New Colors

Today, here and now, is when we embrace the magnificence of who we are. And we look face to face at the powers of the soul—at understanding, imagination, memory, will, and everything else that is part of the life that we are—and gaze upon them with sincere reverence. They have worked together to bring us here, and we love them for what they are, part of our wholeness. They will continue to move, always with greater harmony, to sustain us in Christ consciousness. Because of the divine plan and perfect creation that we are, they will serve more and more fully the cause and effect of love.

Souls in love, you who shine with the light of Heaven and illuminate the Earth in ways that you cannot yet comprehend, I tell you that the tenderness of love will be one of the holy colors of the beautiful rainbow that is the Age of the Heart.

Yes, daughters and sons of the world, sweetness of heart and subtlety of spirit will manifest increasingly. Some of your sisters and brothers will have a more eloquent role than others in manifesting this flower of holiness that is the tenderness of Mary Immaculate. Although not the only ones, some will contribute in a more visible way, as always happens in transitional periods of universal consciousness.

The harshness of yesteryear, the lack of softness, and the aggression that was a false image of strength, will be put aside and give way to the sweet voice of love. I invite you to reflect on this message and make it yours. I call you to be meek and humble of heart, to remain in the unity that you are, in the sweetness of love. In this way your words will reflect the tenderness of God. Your countenance will soften and you will attract all that is holy, beautiful, and perfect.

You show us the importance of Mary's tender grace, a virtue of the soul so closely united to love that you save souls with each demonstration of it. Yes, beloved and beloved of the whole world, each gesture of sweetness that arises from your union with the Immaculate Heart of Mary and the Sacred Heart of Jesus brings Heaven closer to Earth.

When you give an affable smile, a kind look, a serene face, or any of the sweet expressions of peace of which you are capable, you allow divine union to flow from the Source of all creation towards everything. That is how powerful you are, do not forget.

III. The Seal of the New

In this new age that is beginning you will become more and more aware of the power of your souls, and able to honor it. That will allow your light that comes from Christ to manifest freely. You will be living witnesses of the truth that it is not necessary to do great things, but small things with great love.

Remember that the love that you are and Christ consciousness are the same. The new humanity being born— the prelude to the new Heaven and the new Earth—will know that in truth it is not necessary to do anything but to be everything. You will know it is Christ who does and undoes. You will live in peace since as never before you will be attentive to the inner voice.

Those who live in love extend the beauty of holiness because of what they are. This truth will be the guide to lead minds and hearts from now until the end of these times. Nothing will be hidden any more. Everything will come to light. Knowing this will make lies and deceitfulness cease to have the preponderant place they had in past ages.

Everyone will know that they will not be able to hide anything because their inner vision will be restored and because of the clear knowledge of the painful effects caused by a lack of sincerity. The union of love and truth will be recognized for what they are.

Brothers and sisters from all over the universe, men, women, flowers, stars, waters and dolphins, elements of matter and laws that govern material and immaterial creation, I ask all of you to listen carefully: a new end is being written. I call you to accept it in your hearts.

The world will not succumb. Creation will not treat humanity nor any living being with violence or lack of love, for you, beloved humanity, are immersing yourselves more and more in the unfathomable ocean of infinite love, which is Christ consciousness, and your being encompasses all creation.

I ask you, at least for the duration of this dialogue—or even for a moment—to put aside all past associations you have made, learned, or heard about what you call the "apocalypse." That end does not exist because everything that comes from God is eternal. Creations may temporarily misrepresent things, but that need not lead to destruction.

God's tenderness is linked to divine strength. Naturally, this is not something that can be understood by a conflicted mind accustomed to believing that power is separate from love. The end is about the fading away of mental and emotional patterns that are out of harmony with love and truth, which will give way to the full manifestation of the mind of Christ in every living being.

IV. The Novelty of Holy Love

One of the difficulties that the thinking mind has in accepting what is said here is that there exists in you the desire for things to change, the wish that the world you see would be replaced so it may shine as a new world based on love. The other difficulty of the mind is that it is used to thinking in terms of beginnings and endings, having conceived of a Heaven over there and an Earth here. Such difficulties will not last.

The "end" is a concept. There is no truth to it because reality is eternal. God is not fragmented. If there were something like an end to something real, an aspect of God would have to cease to be. That is as impossible as for being to be fragmented. Fragmentation is simply an idea of the mind that perceives itself that way, and then projects its understanding onto life, split from unity.

The subtlety of spirit and delicacy of love will bring all things together in truth. When this occurs everything will be transmuted into light. When universal consciousness is able to fully see the wonders that God created it will be possible for the new Heaven and the new Earth to manifest. The perfect union of the created and the Creator will be recognized. This unity cannot be explained in this work, because what actually happens is beyond all words and symbols. It is a reality beyond description and transcends the purpose of these dialogues.

If you observe what is being revealed in these writings you will realize that you are receiving the knowledge of what already exists but is waiting to be recognized, remembered. In a sense the history of creation is the memory of your consciousness as an effect of the healing of universal memory— the remembrance of God, of truth, of the wonderful reality of creation and its Source.

Since remembrance is simply the seeing of what was previously hidden, denied, or out of sight, it cannot include the idea of destruction. This eliminates the possibility of an end to creation, in which what once was ceases to be. As with a newborn child, beginning to see does not involve destroying or building; it simply is the act of seeing. That is what will happen for everyone. Consciousnesses will be awakened to the truth, and the glory of the Mother and the magnificence of Divine Mercy will be contemplated in all its beauty. The mechanism for denying truth will vanish in the face of this vision, and will be seen for what it is—an attempt to cover the sun with a finger, or to catch the wind with the hands.

My daughters and sons! Let the treasures of the Age of the Heart be expressed by you now and forever so that instead of waiting for it to happen, you, yourselves, will be that era. If you do so, you will take the next natural step: you will realize that you can be Heaven, and that being Heaven is how you restore the light of truth, not only in your own countenance but in the whole world.

Live love now. I am calling you to be the living Christs that you already know you are, and to become established as co-creators of the new. Do not wait. Come to me. Together we will bear witness to the truth as the living expression of God's goodness. And we will allow the sweetness of our hearts to flood the Earth with love.

Blessed are you who receive these words and keep them in the loving silence of your heart.

Thank you for listening to my voice and following it. Thank you for being promoters of the new.

17.

The Role of Truth

I. Acceptance of Light

Daughters and sons of my being, graceful souls, today I come to reveal through this dialogue the benevolence and beauty of truth, as well as its holy function within the plan to return to the consciousness of love, the journey that creation is making towards the Father's house.

Dishonesty, concealment, and everything insincere is the cause of all the evils in the world, including physical and psychological challenges, as well as any type of illness. In a world that lives in truth, there can be nothing but harmony, peace, and joy. The opposite happens in the realm of its absence. If you look carefully at what causes pain in humanity, you will see that it is always something that comes from deception, that which denies the truth.

Denying the truth is the same as denying reality and this can only bring suffering. Do you know why this is so, my love? Yes, you know, because you are a child of light. You do not live in darkness since you remain united to me, and I am the light of true light. Whoever lives consciously in unity with my divine heart lives in the certainty of truth and in the greatness of holiness. In other words, light is made of my being. That is why it is the light of the world.

It has been said that the Age of Reason as well as times previous to it brought much pain to the human family because it lived separated from love. Remember, intelligence without love is cruel. How could it be otherwise, if to deny love is to deny the truth?

A mind disconnected from love plunges into a world of illusions, for only love is real. Here we take a further step towards a greater knowledge of this truth.

Love is the only reality because reality proceeds from, extends, and is, love. There is no reality outside of love because God is the only possible, probable, achievable, and realized reality. There is no more than love and no less. God—the name we give to life and infinite creation—is the only thing in the universe, because His divine reality encompasses everything. God is the All of all. This is the same as saying that love is everything.

II. The Power of Unity

Sisters and brothers of the world, there is no love outside of truth. You have come to co-create and to fulfill an era of new consciousness that we call the Age of the Heart. You do it simply to be who you are. However, in every age it can help one to be fully aware of the signs of the times. This is what these writings seek to impart: the central aspects of the new times in which you are living and which will extend until the advent of the new Earthly Kingdom.

Knowing the signs of the times will give you peace and certainty and eliminate the fear that uncertainty brings. That is why these words are my gift of love. They are given to bring serenity to your life—to know where you are and where you are going.

Beliefs that proclaim that all is lost or that lies will eventually prevail have not yet recognized the power of love and truth. Do not be concerned; lies cannot prevent you from enjoying the infinite power of God. Nothing can destroy Christ, Lord and Mother of all creation. Remember that creation exists for its divine joy and fulfillment in love.

My child, in this truth rests the certainty of the fulfillment of your life and that of the world. It is the foundation of the atonement, the cornerstone of everything

Reality cannot exist outside of love for multiple reasons. Just two of them will be enough for you to begin to change your way of seeing things and completely surrender to the Love of loves. Once you have consciously done so, the light of the living Christ who lives in you will shine with a luminosity as never before. Its brilliance will attract countless beings to the light of truth.

One reason it is impossible for there to be a reality outside of love is that something foreign to love would have no laws that could support it. Reality can only exist by virtue of the laws that sustain it. A reality without law is inconceivable. Not even humans can come together as a family without laws that somehow unite and support it. The same is true of the laws of creation. Reality and the law to which it belongs are a unit.

From a consciousness asleep to love, nothing can arise but a sleeping intelligence. In such a state, the true mental faculties—and with it the soul—remain inert, like a seed that cannot germinate. Thus, the effects that arise from it are disharmonious with love. Think of the melodies sung by a choir. For it to exist in its entirety, each and every voice needs to sing as intended. Otherwise it will go out of tune or be incomplete. Something similar happens with the powers of the soul.

III. The Concert of the Soul

Living in harmony is living a concerted life, one in which everything moves to the rhythm, time, and direction that corresponds to it according to the laws that give it existence. If this does not occur, it goes against its foundation.

The law of love, being God Himself, gives sustenance and existence to reality. Just as there is no distance between the created and the Creator, neither is there between the law, its cause, its reality, and its effect. When it was said that God wrote His commandments on the human heart, what is meant is that His law, His divine being, and what you are, are the same. This is why you cannot live without love; without love you would cease to be, since there would be no supporting laws.

You may think you can be a lawmaker apart from God, but that is not true. Only love can create laws, because love is the only creative source, and outside of love nothing can be created since there is nothing outside of love.

Humanity's "laws," particularly in the recent era, are simply an externalization of fearful thoughts. That is not law, although it finds its source in the innate knowledge that law is necessary.

Can love give rise to laws for the world's functioning? Yes, of course, and it will increasingly do so. Even many human laws come from love. Child of my heart, there is no reason that the laws governing your life cannot come from love. That is simply a matter of where you decide to dwell: in love or in fear, in truth or in illusion.

Beloveds of Heaven, in the Age of the Heart love will embrace the world's functional systems in a greater way than previously. This will not arise as a human adjustment to human laws, but as the effect of a new state of consciousness.

I invite you and the world to live consciously subject to the law of love right now, allowing it to be the only source of your knowledge and actions. By doing so, you allow the embrace of love to hover over the world's laws. It starts with you, and eventually extends to everyone and everything. When the ability to enact laws and count on them is returned to love, humanity will have returned to truth and will find peace.

Another reason for the impossibility of a reality outside of love is that God is love. Although this statement may not seem to have great relevance to everyday life, it actually permeates all of human existence. If God is love and also infinite—and I assure you that this is true—where could a reality separate from Him dwell, except in nothingness?

IV. In the Mind of Christ

Nothingness and the whole have been moving in the human mind and heart as if they were the sources of a duality that has governed the history of creation. And they will continue to be a fundamental part of the dual Earthly Kingdom until the achievement of the Second Advent of Christ, in which love will come in all its glory and establish a fullness born of divine love to the new Heaven and the new Earth.

Outside of love is nothing. The only options to choose from are nothing or everything, illusion or truth. Nothing arouses fear; love awakens and gives away everything. It has always been like this in the world of form. You can choose freely. You hold the choice for love, and with it, Christ consciousness. This choice is how you dwell in the abode of the living and extend reality to all creation.

You certainly can and should extend reality. This is the same as extending your being. Be aware, souls full of kindness, that reality is what you are because you are love. Reality lies in the truth of what you are. This knowledge will be accepted more and more until it becomes the certainty that governs the world. This will happen in the Age of the Heart. When joyfully recognized, duality will give way to the perpetual union of love. Promoting that is the role of truth, and your role.

You cannot live in reality if you do not live in the truth of your being because reality is God, and only God is the Source and existence of your being and of all being.

Now we go deeper into the mind of Christ and step forward into the vast ocean of truth. We recognize that to live in ways in which you are not yourself is to live a crazy life. This is the only definition of madness that could apply to you. Do not look for another, although for some there may be.

Not being truly what you are is insanity. You do that every time you fail to remain united with what you are in the present moment, which disconnects you from me, the Christ in you. That is the history of humanity: attempts to establish that which is not and cannot be because it does not have laws that support it. This should not be cause for concern, but for rest. What never was will forever cease to be for it has no basis upon which to exist. And it won't be around for much longer. The lie must come to an end. The Age of the Heart is its harbinger, a prelude to the plenitude of love.

Remember then, my child, that your being is the gateway to reality because God dwells there. At its center resides the law of love, the foundation of all true law. Make this the only source of your knowledge and work, and you will be bringing the Kingdom of Heaven to Earth, for love is Heaven itself.

Make love your guide, your support, and your livelihood. Do this and you will live in perfect harmony with the truth, for indeed love is what sustains you and the entire universe.

I tell you truly that as a result of this you will receive eternal life, in alignment with the treasures of perfect love. You will forever enjoy the wonders that God created for you.

Do you realize how important it is to become aware of your direct relationship with God? Do you understand that in it resides the joy of your soul, its fulfillment and fullness? Of course you understand, otherwise you would not have allowed my voice to reach you, nor would you be receiving these words full of life and goodness. And because you know it and you bring it to consciousness through your union with these words, universal consciousness is illuminated more and more with the light of truth.

Giving and receiving are one, just as truth, reality, being, and love are one.

Blessed are you, who listen to my voice and follow it.

Rest in peace.

18.

The Voice of God

I. The Great Transformation

Beloved soul of my divine being, here we are again, bearing witness to our union, in which all true meaning dwells. We are relationship. We are whole, expressing ourselves in form. We are created and creative love, the endless source of life.

I have said that the Great Transformation of the world, which will come about in the attainment of the new Earthly Kingdom, will take place through consciousness and nothing else. It would be an error to believe that the changes that humanity senses are necessary—which come from an innate knowledge—will come about as a result of ideas of the thinking mind based on what has been learned in the past, or by observation of the present.

There is an eternal, unavoidable union between what is and its expression, between the unmanifested and manifestation. In that union lies the foundation of the world's existence and of all creation. Unmanifested being is a way of not being.

The extension of who you are is essential to being yourself. The following experience will help you understand: your heart feels anxiety and fear, but you do not know its cause. Suddenly, you allow your being to express, whereupon peace begins to return to your soul, fear leaves, and love shines.

My love, in that example you are not denying feelings of fear or doing anything but sincerely expressing your being. You allow your being to express itself in harmony with what it really is feeling. An example of this is that you are here, receiving and giving shape to our dialogues of love and holiness. Is it not true that your heart rejoices and feels peace when it hears my voice? Is it true, beloved of my heart, that there is a serene joy in the soul when it spends time with its Divine Creator, Source, destination, and purpose? What is this about?

Every human soul has the ability to hear the voice of their Mother-Father God. This ability is inherent in every creature. Truly I tell you that each animal, plant, rock, and even each element that constitutes matter can hear my voice according to its particular way of being. All hear the sweet voice of love calling them permanently into existence. How else could they exist?

II. My Voice Will Be Heard

God said let there be light and there was light. And with it came everything else. How could something like that happen if light does not have the ability to hear and follow the divine voice? The same happens with your being. You exist as an effect of having answered the call of love in the moment of your creation, to remain in existence forever, to enjoy eternal life. When love called you to participate in the banquet of life, you responded, "Your will be done." And Her will was done. That is why you exist. And you remain forever in union with God. For She—and only She—can call beings into life.

Loved ones from all corners of the world, listen carefully. The voice of God—the Source of life and the foundation of reason and the heart—sustains all things in existence. Her Word is present here, now, and always. She is never absent from reality, the ultimate reality of being, its cause and expression. Do not be surprised when I tell you these things. In the past, humanity believed that only a few could hear my voice calling them to eternal life. But that is a thing of the past. There is no room for such belief in the new consciousness which is now present.

Again, a central aspect of the Age of the Heart is the conscious manifestation of a direct relationship with God. Human spirits— an expression of creation—return to the original state of direct communication with the Creator, which, being the state of unity, is the only natural and real way of living.

For the purposes of this work, we will define unconsciousness as the loss or decrease of the ability to hear the voice of love. This expression is not simply symbolic; it points directly to the truth. The inner noise of the soul, the result of the denial of being, caused it to be unable to hear love's serene voice clearly, or even at all, despite being active in every living being. This is why the Holy Spirit has played such an essential role in the atonement. Its divine reality is what makes, and will always make, the soul listen to the voice of Christ. If the soul cannot do it fully because of the daze it is in, the Holy Spirit listens for it, responding eternally to the call of life.

The separate mind—so attached to arguing and explaining everything—could argue that if it is the Holy Spirit and not the soul that listens and responds when it experiences difficulty hearing God because of its bewilderment, then it is not listening properly. But, my beloved souls who embrace wisdom, this is inaccurate. You and the Holy Spirit united. How the Holy Spirit answers is the response of your soul as well.

III. Life Is Union

There is no distance between the Holy Spirit—which is the essence of God and also the essence of Jesus—and you. It knows you from all eternity, and knows the perfect unity in which all creation rests in peace. It also knows the uniqueness in which each creature has been created as a holy expression of divine will. It is the bridge between the human and the Divine, the unifying power of human and divine nature in Christ, the union of the created and the Creator.

There is no separation between the Holy Spirit and Christ, just as there is no separation between creation and its Source. Distancing is alien to the realm of love. Love draws the loved one to itself, making them one. The space that separates forms is perceived as something that actually separates only by a mind that wishes to deny the unity of love. But those who have found the truth, and that includes you who receive these words and all those who are part of this expression, know that physical distance is simply the means that love has arranged so that everyone one can meet each other in their uniqueness, thereby knowing and making God known in the one and the whole.

Once the inner noise subsides sufficiently, the soul returns to the state of communion, living inspired by the voice of Christ and united to it without interruption. When the soul has reached that state, the Holy Spirit sinks into divine silence. Beforehand It acts as an interpreter. Thus there is a time between the soul regaining the ability to hear the voice of God and putting what that voice says into words. This not only occurs in each one of my beloved brothers and sisters, but in universal consciousness.

Interpreting the voice from Heaven that is spoken in each soul is a matter for the divine spirit, until the ability of simultaneous translation is restored in the soul. To understand this, think about the example of learning a new language. First you need to hear it and have someone explain it to you. Then you "think" in relation to that language. You need time between the appearance of the desire to express something in that language, and the ability to find the right word. Over time, by simple repetition, the new language is incorporated into your mind. You no longer need interpreters or interpretation mechanisms. You do it automatically. You begin to think and feel in that language. Language has been integrated. This also occurs with the language of love.

Humanity is moving towards the state in which the voice of truth, which is that of love, is accepted as the only source of knowing and acting. I assure you, soul full of light, the day will come when everyone will recognize my voice and will follow it. Every day there are more, and the number will continue to grow. Hear me with holy grace, for I tell you truly that more and more sisters and brothers—and other aspects of creation—will join these dialogues of union and truth.

IV. A New Portal to Love

This work is a new portal. It is an expression of a new dialogue that Heaven has opened with Earth—new and yet eternal at the same time. The fulfillment of the promises given to humanity will take place within. I invite you all to be part of that reality now. Remember that life and creation are an unceasing dialogue of love and truth, which is why these writings constitute a call to life without end.

Beloveds from all corners of the universe, if you enjoy the thinking mind, if you enjoy the sentient aspect of human nature, I call you to remain in constant dialogue with the source of knowledge. In it you will find the answer to every question. You will enjoy the only knowing that is in harmony with who you are. You will witness, or actually remember, that total dependence on Divine Love is an essential part of your nature, for it is what you are. I will explain.

Everything you and all creation needs to be full and fulfill the happy purpose of your existence as God has ordained is provided by your Creator. No divine creation is self-sustaining. There is no need for it to be. This applies to both the material and immaterial dimensions.

Look at the cypress tree. Behold its majesty. Does it not depend on the sun and rain given by the Creator for the simple reason of love? Where does it get its food if not from the soil that God gives freely? Can you see how each living being receives according to its nature so that it can be realized and exist fully according to its unique way of being? If this is so for the cypress and the birds of the sky, how could it be different for you?

Beloved sons and daughters, enter into the dialogue of creation where we dwell together in love and holiness. Enter and remain there always. I assure you that you will hear things that fill your hearts with love, your minds with peace, and your souls with wonder. In this dialogue you will find everything you need to be happy. You will be freed from the endless false needs of the world that ended up drowning you and taking away your freedom. You will know the truth. And you will be captivated by the love that you are, a love without beginning or end.

Love our conversations. Honor our holy dialogues. Allow Heaven to flood your life now and forever so that God's dream may come true in you. Let go of your interpretations about everything. Empty yourself of identification with your desires, feelings, thoughts, and history. You are not that. What you really are is beyond all human reasoning, something you know well.

I lovingly remind you that only within the dialogue that exists between the Creator and the created is it possible to know each other in the light of truth, as well as to know all things as they are. This is because dialogue is unity and reality as God has created it.

V. Reality and Fullness

To know yourself outside of what is real is to know yourself in illusion, which is not knowledge. This is why I tell you that you can only know yourself in me, your beloved Christ, your source and your life. United we are reality. We can only meet in love. This knowledge is spreading more and more until it will embrace the whole Earth. From it will emerge a new world whose foundation is truth.

Just as the birds of the sky and the lilies of the field neither sow nor reap and yet lack nothing, so humanity has begun now in the Age of the Heart to embrace the freedom that comes with a life of simplicity. Humanity's load will be lighter as it walks the roads of the world. It will be more and more detached from earthly things. It will cease to be moved by greed, which for so long has plunged it into the tyranny of fear. It will experience how abundantly the love of God provides, as it was at the beginning of all beginnings. It will cease earning its daily bread by the sweat of its brow because it will be given as directly as a loving mother feeds her child.

You will be witnesses of what is said here. You will see how humanity will decide increasingly for a simple life, a life of freedom. This will occur not as a result of a new mental tendency, but as the effect of a new state of consciousness in which men and women around the world will recognize that their worth is not related to their possessions but to the holiness in which they were created.

The call to accumulate, which is the fruit of the fear of not being, will be ignored; the mind and heart will instead hear the voice of God. They will join in the continual dialogue full of purity that takes place within the soul. By joining this dialogue you will recognize that it is not just an expression of communion, but is the place—which is not a place—in which Christ and your being dwell in peace. And it is where your being remains united with perfect love, being eternally one with everything and at the same time forever unique. There, the self and the being intermingle in a dance of light. They move to the beat of eternal life, their source. All this will be vividly experienced by the new humanity that is being born, and which little by little is populating the Earth for the glory of Heaven.

Rest in the certainty of my love.

19.

Mother of Christ

I. The Divine Unity

Blessed soul of the Father, you who receive these words, ensconce yourself within my sweet heart. Take refuge in me. Make the grace of my Divine Love yours, for that it is. Do not allow anguish, sadness, and fear to nest in you. When they appear, embrace them and give them to me. I will transform them into joy, song, and greater knowledge of the love of the Mother-Father God who lives in you. Rest in the stillness of our holy encounter, here where sweetness dwells, and the beauty of our union envelops all that we are.

Today I have come to remind you—and through you the whole world—that union with Christ, which is the goal of the human soul and of all creation, is achieved in union with Mary, mother of all creation. Just as a child needs a father and a mother to be conceived, so it is with the human Christ. You have always had a heavenly Mother and an eternal Father. Both are inseparable—not two different beings that relate to each other, but one. Both aspects can be distinguished but not separated.

One of the signs of the new consciousness, or the Age of the Heart, is the significant relevance that Mother Mary has and will have. Integration of her being is necessary prior to achievement of the Kingdom of Christ on Earth because only in her does truth and unity exist.

To love Mary is to love Jesus. To love both is to love Christ. In other words, it is to love what you are and what everything really is, since the source of being resides in the Mary-Jesus union. This does not occur only because they are role models but rather that this perfect union is one with you.

Just as you cannot separate light from the sun or heat from fire, you cannot separate what you are from Christ. And since Jesus and Mary are the unity that Christ is, your being cannot disconnect from it and exist.

To melt in love is to become one with truth. This will be understood more and more in these new times until it is accepted on all levels. Humanity will go deeper and deeper into this mystery until this becomes part of its knowledge. From this integration, peace will be born in all hearts and harmony will reign in the world.

You who receive these words, it is as important as breathing is for the life of the body that you consecrate yourself to the love of Mary. This does not mean that you have to create sides or develop a belief that causes disputes or separations; that is not part of the unity of love.

What is being said, my children, is that the Divine Maternity is the Source of the birth of Christ in the realm of time just as that same motherhood, made flesh as Mother Mary, gave birth to Christ in human nature and took the form of a physical man. So too will Christ be conceived in every living creature. And it will be the purest womb of Mary's love that performs this miracle—a mystery of infinite love.

To immerse yourself day after day in the love of the Mother of the living, of your Heavenly Mother, is necessary in these times so full of grace and blessing. Remember that you are living at a time in history when Heaven and Earth are coming together as never before, not only now, but in every moment from the beginning of the Age of the Heart to the full establishment of the new Earthly Kingdom.

II. The Totality of Being

Beloveds from all over the world, it is in Mary that you will find the fullness of Christ and in her Immaculate Heart that you will be able to know yourselves as God knows you. There is no Jesus without Mary, nor Mary without Jesus. This needs to be accepted with joy and peace for the full beauty of Christ to be realized in your consciousness. Creation was born from the love of the Divine Father and Mother, the union of Divine Motherhood with the fecundating Spirit that dwells in divinity.

You were not born from nothing. You were born as an act of love, not from a union of equals but as an inseparable extension of divine unity. Within the being of God is creative potentiality that makes Mother-Father God a Creator and allows creation to exist. That divine power creates from the union of the two realities of the eternal being. One is the reality of conceiving, the other that of fertilizing. From that perfect and eternal union arises creation forever. Similarly, the new creation will be born of the unity of Christ, which consists of the undivided union of the Sacred Heart of Jesus and the Immaculate Heart of Mary.

Do not be afraid of losing yourself in your love for the Mother of Heaven and Earth. All love that you profess to her, you are professing to Christ. The more you let yourself be loved by her, the more ardent love you will feel for Christ. This love of Mary arises not only through religious devotion, for love is universal. Every time you love peace, harmony, beauty, sweetness of heart, purity of spirit, the wisdom of love, and total obedience to love, you are expressing your love for Mary and you are loving Christ.

Loving your brothers and sisters, loving yourself and all creation in the love of God is how you make the truth about who you are shine on Earth as it is in Heaven. Remember: the only essential thing is love. In this dialogue I am inviting you to remain united to the source of holy love which is the Immaculate Heart of Mary, to let you love her. With that you will be absorbed by a love without beginning or end. You will fall in love with your Mother-Father God to such a degree that your humanity will be the perfect reflection of eternal happiness. You will be the living face of joy without end and a beauty without opposite.

Let yourself be loved by Mary more each day. Make it not only an intention but a way of life. I ask you to meditate serenely on this message, for it represents the simplest way to bring Heaven to Earth. This path will speed up your achievement of the Second Advent and your fullness. This path avoids steep, tiring, and unnecessary byways.

III. The Mother Cradles

I invite you, my sisters and brothers, to follow this safe, simple, and level path of letting yourself be loved by Mary. Allow Her to lead your soul, your humanity, and your reality. You will obtain the grace and joy of consciously co-creating the new Earthly Kingdom. You will heal yourself and others. You will light up the world. You will fill your existence with beauty, as well as that of all creation.

Through this path given to you here you will know the love of God as never before. You will feel not of the world but of Heaven, intoxicated by a force as serene as it is powerful, the power of immaculate love through which the Earth and all creatures are sanctified, just as was the divine incarnation in human form.

Don't be carried away by the fear of religious symbols or the habit of separation through dogmatism. Remain in the depths of your soul, for it knows the truth. It knows that what is said here arises from the wisdom of Heaven. Remember that in every heart is a deep desire to reach the truth and an irrepressible impulse towards beauty and goodness.

When you allow that inner force coming from the essential power of the soul to be satisfied by being transformed into action, then you achieve freedom as the children of God—the highest aspiration of your humanity and of all creation.

Your union with the Immaculate Heart of Mary, always united to the Sacred Heart of Jesus, will give you full awareness of your true identity as most holy sons and daughters of your Mother-Father God and the knowledge that allows you to live as what you really are, the human-Christ. This knowledge is the destiny of your holy mind and the aspiration of your heart. Getting there is possible, though not by solitary means.

On the plane of truth, nothing can be achieved alone. Creation is totally of union. The whole remains eternally united to everything and to everyone in the harmony of holiness and the truth of being.

Rest in the arms of Mary. Rest in her Immaculate Heart. Join her all the days of your life. I assure you that you will see your humanity transform into light, beauty, and holiness beyond what you can imagine. You will take flight.

Unite right now and forever with a love that has no beginning or end, a love in which you are as you were created to be. And let it be the Heaven of your holy mind and the purity of your heart united to Christ that shape your life. In doing so you will give the world the greatest treasure: you will be bringing Heaven to Earth. You will be making the new Earthly Kingdom shine in all its glory. And above all you will give yourselves the joy of living in the fullness of love.

I bless you in truth.

20.

Life Without End

I. The Eternal Brightness of Being

My child, soul born of the love of God, you who surrender to the flow of inspiration to receive and give these words, I have to tell you that a great light is illuminating minds. A constant flow of grace and blessing is moving from the heart of the Mother of the living towards every aspect of creation.

Today I come to remind you that death does not exist. This truth is so essential that I cannot stop reminding you of it as often as necessary, due to the forgetful nature of the thinking mind. Deep down in your heart, you know this is true and that it is impossible for there to be death or any annihilation of who you are. You have been created with that knowing. You are perfectly aware that everything that comes from God is eternal, since everything that exists resembles its Source.

"Dying" is but a loving step that each one who temporarily inhabits the Earth takes in due time to begin living the true life. At no other time are those beings more active in love. Truly I tell you, they are more alive than ever. You can feel this truth in your heart. It is experienced in various ways. One of them is the peace that your heart feels. Another is the deep silence that envelops your soul and your desire to remember loved ones. In many other ways the truth is revealed that eternal life exists and is the destiny of every living being.

What happens at death? The ties are unbound that made it impossible for the soul to love with perfect love, whereupon it returns to the state in which it is capable of living in love and letting the self be loved perfectly.

The drama of humanity is not knowing how to love with perfect love. Humans want to love but cause hurt. They want to live in peace but wage war. They want to be happy but do things that love would never do and thereby create their own unhappiness. Why? What is it that drives the human family to such incongruous behavior?

There exists in the human soul—and in every creature that inhabits the plane of time, space and matter, both animate and inanimate—an acquired condition that prevents it from living freely in the unity of love. It matters not what you call that condition—separation, original sin, alien will, insanity, and so on—all that matters is that you accept that it has been acquired and is not inherent in divine creation.

Because it is acquired and not created, it can be modified. Indeed, the entire history of temporal, spatial, and material creation has that as its purpose. That purpose is achieved because every purpose founded on truth always achieves realization.

II. The Road of Life

The ultimate goal of the material universe is to have all of creation return to the Father's house, to the one love that exists in all things, the only reality. Who has arranged this to be so? God Himself, the sole Source of meaning. Be glad that it is so.

Once the path has been completed that leads the human soul to detach from everything that prevented it from loving and letting itself be perfectly loved without limitation, then it has completed what you call the "path of life"—an expression which is inadequate if it refers only to the material human experience. The path of life is eternal because it is love. Outside of love there is no path, no life. In it resides all bliss, fulfillment, and existence in truth.

All perfect wisdom dwells in love. All indescribable joy dwells in love. Every life is full and forever happy. In God's plan, in true life, the notion of death is both inconceivable and absurd. Human beliefs have tried to give different descriptions of what a true life is, but that does not make them true. What makes these words given here true from God's Heaven and for all humanity is my resurrection.

For centuries I have said that I defeated death. I will continue saying it until it is no longer necessary to do so. Nevertheless, many of you have not changed your beliefs much around this transition to eternal life.

I invite you to absorb these words into your hearts and become one with them. Allow the truth of which they remind you to illuminate your minds and embrace your hearts. Feel how much peace and joy it gives you to know for sure that your loved ones who have already completed the path of Earth and have taken a tiny step towards the holy abode, are much closer to you than ever, more active in love, and more alive than you can imagine. They are part of your lives as much as they were when you could see them with your eyes.

When someone goes into the next room, do they cease to exist? Sisters and brothers, I am calling you to be embodiments of the Age of the Heart. To do so it is necessary to begin to live the truth in all its breadth. One aspect is to recognize that life is eternal because it comes from God, and that death does not exist.

You may wonder why we speak of "true life," as if its existence were not possible. I do this to distinguish a life lived in truth from one that is not so lived. A true life is not being lived if you are unable to love with perfect love and are not fully capable of letting yourself be loved infinitely with a love without measure, a love that has no beginning or end, a life-giving love that cheers the soul and floods all creation with beauty, happiness, and indescribable gratitude, uninterruptedly and ever increasingly.

Life is fullness, sincere joy, and endless purity. It has no opposite, no force that can dominate the soul or prevent it from loving and being loved with perfect love in the holiness of truth.

III. The Body as a Portal to the Truth

My daughters and sons, once the path outlined in the human experience of time has been completed, one passes to a conscious state in which the fullness of holy love is the only reality. The transition to the glory of God has been made in which all knowledge is given constantly, effortlessly, to the mind.

Likewise, all peace and all the treasure of the Kingdom is granted to the heart in endless abundance. Being shines forth in all its magnificence, without distractions, obstructions, or limitations. There you are as you were created to be eternally, and that is why you are happier than you are can imagine and more alive than ever.

Note that I said "once the path outlined in the human experience of time has been completed." This is because the state of union with truth, in which one lives in perfect love, can be realized on the earthly path. The bodily experience need not limit love. Therefore, it is not necessary to wait, although normally souls take their time to get there.

Blessed soul, you who live submerged in the light—which is why you receive these words here and now—you must know that in the Age of the Heart beliefs about death will be quite different from those of the Age of Reason and of previous eras. Yet some beliefs are preserved, especially those that concern respect, honor, and remembering in holiness those for whom Divine Love formed part of the earthly path; those already enjoy the freedom of the daughters and sons of God.

Increasingly, the lack of distance between Heaven and Earth will be accepted. A new way of understanding and living the transition to the glory of life will emerge.

The belief that eternal life is over there and a temporary life is here, separate aspects of reality, is typical of past ages. In the new consciousness that is already here, that of the Second Advent, it is understood—through the consciousness of Christ in you—that it is simply not true.

Today we let go of that way of thinking forever without judging it and without longing for a familiar past that is untrue, since it is unreal. We open ourselves now to be graced with the revelation of Heaven. We let ourselves be filled with Divine Love. We allow our Divine Mother to guide us and show us the truth. We keep silent. We receive God.

Why do we bring this knowledge here? Because if you still believe in death as reality, you are not fully embracing the truth. Death does not exist because it is not real. There is only life, for God is the only reality from Whose holiness all reality extends eternally in perfect love, eternal truth, and endless bliss. Repeat this expression of holy wisdom as often as necessary until you have made it real in yourself. Above all, receive it in your pure heart, full of joy and gratitude.

Daughters and sons of the world, be assured that love will gather within itself everyone and everything, and that in this holy gathering we will eternally sing praises to Divine Glory and feel a joy that will never end. Hold this truth as a vital force that moves you every day, every hour, every moment. In it dwells the truth, I assure you. By having his light accompany you, you walk with Christ, who is the truth and the life.

With love, I tell you that you will receive many graces because you have eagerly accepted this revelation, not as blind acceptance of a new doctrine, but from immersing yourself in the deep silence of your heart, and allowing the eternal wisdom that dwells in your holy mind to reveal the truth. Accordingly, you will know that in the end the only thing left is love, and with it, holiness, eternal life, perfect purity, the beauty of truth, and the fullness of being.

I bless you in peace.

21.

The Ark of Life

I. Rejoining in Consciousness

Soul full of light! You who live under the protection of love, you who have made love your refuge, your strength, and the source of your knowledge and work, know that you are never alone. The peace of Christ accompanies you wherever you go, along with his holiness, his love, and all that is holy in God's infinite creation. The angels fill your life with joy, sowing flowers of purity and truth with your every step.

Sensitive souls who are receiving these words! You who tirelessly seek to lift the veil that stands between the thinking mind and the wisdom of Christ, you are my heart's co-creators of the new Earthly Kingdom because you know that eternal truth exists.

My divinity dwells in you and with it everything that is real in the immeasurable created universe. Every star in the firmament belongs to you, every petal of every flower, every song of every bird, every ray of sunshine, and every one of your brothers and sisters. The angels too are yours, as is the Divine Mother.

Today I come so that together we can reveal the matter of healing. It was said that this theme would be developed in due time. Now is that time. Being aware of the need for healing is a grace and a blessing. Indeed, it is only possible in a consciousness enlightened enough to see beyond the surface of the world to the underlying truth. Not all creatures are aware of it. Why?

You, as conscious beings endowed with a human nature, are the ones who have the power, in union with me, to gather creation within your hearts in divine union. You are, so to speak, the collectors of creation. God in you is linked to the truth to a much greater degree than you can imagine.

Love—the source of life, reason, and being—is what calls and sustains everything in existence. Each in existence has its function, its holy purpose, though different in form and therefore different in the way each fulfills its creative purpose. This can be easily understood if it is recognized that God does nothing in vain. He did not create you "just because;" neither did God create the countless grains of sand randomly.

Everything exists in union with the divine purpose of spreading love eternally. Thus it is necessary for everything to remain in perpetual union with its Source. This is true not as an imposition, but because it is life and being.

II. Holy Creators

Only love can create more love. Only love can create. The rest is pure illusion.

Fantasies may seem to create powerful images, or rather ghosts, to fabricate a reality parallel to truth, but in due time they will vanish in the blink of an eye. Reality is eternal; it cannot fade.

You are real because you are my child. I am real because I am the truth, reality itself, and nothing true exists outside of me. I have said that only love is real. I ask you, my beloved, to hold this true statement on high during this dialogue of love and holiness.

It will help you understand the magnificence of your purpose in life—not only in what you call eternal life but also in the life of form and time, since both are a unit.

You were created with a certain consciousness. This is what makes you have a human soul and not something else. Human identity is a gift from Heaven given to you in your creation because God always intended for you to participate in His divinity. This is why you possess the consciousness you have, the mind you have, and the heart you have. Every part of you is perfect because of God's purpose for you.

There is no need to change anything about who you are. Everything about you has the capacity to gather within yourself what you are in Christ. You have the ability to bring and hold in Heaven all creation, as well as yourself. You do this every time you remain in the truth of what you are, that is, in love.

Beloved of my being, listen with loving attention to what I tell you now, and treasure it:

You are a holy heart capable of embracing everyone and
everything in love. Creation returns and remains in
divine reality through humanity.

Without this occurring there is no eternal meeting of love, no banquet of life. Just as I gather within myself all humanity in God, you gather all creation within yourself in me.

Can you begin to understand what I am talking about? Can you now realize that my purpose and yours are identical? We are both the ark of life within which every living being is called to dwell in the bliss of beautiful love and the eternal reality of God. This ark is not to protect us from a deluge, but for all to reunite in the purity of holiness and unending joy.

III. The Universe Embraced

Beloveds of Heaven and all creation! The image of an ark is not large enough to embrace the scope of your heart's feeling towards all creation, since despite its clear meaning, it represents a limitation.

Within the embrace of divine love which extends from my heart to yours, and from it to the entire universe, all creatures are drawn and gathered in union. Within it everyone enjoys Heaven eternally in all its unlimited scope, width and length.

Blessed soul that hears my voice, just as one day I extended my arms to attract everyone to the gathering of saints, you are attracting all creation due to the radiant light that flows from the center of your heart to all creation.

I assure you that the luminescence, warmth, and beauty of each ray reaches every created thing. Everything benefits. The brilliance of your light is unlimited. Its beauty is without compare. It contains everything that healing and sustenance require. Where it is accepted—not by the thinking mind but in the depths of the heart—peace, health, joy, and knowledge of truth enter.

I shine on you with all my glory and you shine on all creation with a light that is never extinguished and knows no limit. Our light has unlimited range because it is the light of life. Perhaps many do not feel or perceive that they are embraced by the rays of light that spring from our unity. This is of no essential importance, since the truth need not be understood nor accepted to be what it is.

You came into the world with the purpose of attracting all creation to yourself through the light of your holiness, and to return to each one of my daughters and sons what one day was taken from me, which includes every aspect of the material universe. Perhaps this statement surprises you, or you may consider it hyperbole, but I assure you it is not.

I do nothing alone; I do everything with you. For that I gave you the heart you have, one capable of knowing God and going beyond what is apparent to the truth that sustains everything. That is why I have also given you a mind in which the truth can dwell freely and in peace. For the same reason you have been given the being that you are, one capable of merging with Christ in such a way that there is no longer any distance from your Source.

Meditate on this.

22.

Full of Love

I. Universal Healing

Blessed soul of the Mother, child of light that shines at all times and places, I have said that we will speak of the need for healing as it pertains to consciousness. Being aware of the need for healing is itself healing. There may seem to be a time before one feels the effect of healing, but that is a matter of perception. To put it plainly, none can heal unconsciously, because the denial of the consciousness of what you are is the source of the lack of wholeness.

To heal is to gather in love. What else can keep consciousness healthy, and with it the soul, if not the truth? You may not believe that living in love and truth is the source of healing and the sustenance of a healthy state, but if you look around the world a bit, you can observe that this is so, even in the realm of delusion.

Living in love is living in the truth of who you are; it keeps you within the embrace of holiness. Those who remain there receive the light of life in their minds, hearts, and consciousness—in all their humanity, allowing divine energy to flood every aspect of them and for them to remain "safe and sound."

My child, the definition of illness will change in the Age of the Heart, until it includes Christ in this understanding. The universal consciousness of the created was not always capable of conceiving the idea that one could be sick nor that disease was curable. We have already spoken of this. In the new consciousness dawning, everyone will understand that healing is necessary. This knowledge will be universal, so you will see more and more people looking to live in healthy ways. Naturally, this is achieved as an effect of consciousness.

Until very recently, disease was thought to exist when abnormal functioning of the body manifested itself. That notion extended to the mind and what you call mental illnesses. Disease came to be conceived of as a malfunction of some aspect of the psychosomatic human being. This was a great advance, the effect of a state of consciousness that humanity simply could not conceive of before that time.

In the Age of the Heart, humanity will take a step forward in the global concept of disease. It will get to the root of things, not by deduction or because of a discovery by the thinking mind, but as an inevitable consequence of a new state of consciousness. Everyone will know—or rather will remember—that health is achievable as a natural state of being. This will be innate knowledge. And humanity will recognize that health is fully realized only by remaining united to the source of beautiful love.

Living in truth and love will cease merely sounding good, merely a high ideal. It will become the essential rule governing life on Earth. Once again, this will not come about as a deduction, but as a natural consequence of the loving consciousness in which creation—including humanity—has entered.

II. Unity: Source of Wholeness

I have said that healing is reuniting in love and is engraved in the heart of every living being. All incompleteness comes from a separated state of consciousness. It is the effect of a particular degree of unity. When the unity of being with God and therefore with everyone and everything in Christ is denied, the doors open to an experience contrary to the fullness of love. Naturally, this will manifest itself in multiple ways, all of which carry the same consequence: suffering.

In the vision of Christ, disease is everything that causes suffering. It can be a misconception, a situation, or a condition. If you deny joy, peace, and happiness from your present moment, Heaven looks at it as something requiring healing.

According to the criteria of the old you can have a healthy body; yet if you do not live in the truth you are not complete and in the view of Christ consciousness, the life-giving grace of healing is required. In the past the idea of illness was reserved for the body and later became incorporated into the mental and psychic aspects. Now it will take another step: it will incorporate consciousness.

A healthy consciousness supports a healthy mind and a healthy body. Let us now replace the word consciousness with heart. A healthy heart radiates the life force of Christ to all creation, including the body, the mind, and the universe.

But what is a healthy consciousness? What is a healthy heart? A healthy consciousness is one that does not deny any aspect of being. In it everything is embraced in the light. It leaves nothing of what you are outside of yourself. A healthy heart loves all things with the only love that is true, the love of your Mother-Father God. It does so when it renounces itself and remains empty of everything, to be filled only by Christ— only by God's will.

Giving up the desire to have a separate will from God is healing because it is giving up the separation that is the source of all incompleteness. This knowledge will be accepted by humanity as an effect of the new consciousness and will be lived with joy. We can say, without fear of falling into reductionism, that this will be the foundation of the new Heaven and the new Earth, because the foundations of the eternal life of Heaven rest upon it.

Be glad you made it this far. Up to the point in which both individual and universal consciousness begin to remember that health is the natural state of the sons and daughters of God, there are no reasons not to live that way, with love being the source of all healing.

I tell you with all the love in my heart to give up your ideas of separation. Drop all your interpretations about what you think things are and what you want them to be. Free yourself now from the burden on your shoulders, the belief that it is you who have to define what you are or what others are. Give up forever the desire to know anything for yourself. Empty yourself of everything. The more you do so, the more love will fill you.

How can you do that? Let yourself be loved. Stay consciously in our union always. Pour out your heart on me. Tell me everything, then rest in the peace that comes from knowing that I will take care of everything.

Be silent with me often. Let my voice reach you. I am the love that has no beginning or end. I am the source of healing, the origin and destiny of life. I am the Christ in you. Whoever remains in me is already in eternal life. And above all, remember that we are but a thought away from each other. With a simple "I love you" to me, you bring Heaven to Earth.

Be glad be creation.

23.

Awakeners of Being

I. True Knowledge

Beloved children, blessed souls, daughters and sons from all over the world, today I come clothed in the glory that belongs to me by right, and is yours gratuitously. Everything of mine is yours because that is how I have arranged it. I am perfect love; therefore I give myself completely. Whoever receives me, receives the divinization of humanity as a blessed gift for their sincere desire for union with my divinity.

You may have thought you were other than indoctrination of the world, other than what you really are. Still, despite its attempt to tame you, mundane reality never succeeded.

Everyone carries within themselves the knowledge of who they really are. Although it not easily put into words, an inner force drives you to recognize who you really are. We have already discussed this, but we mention it again so that you understand that the true way of the world is the realization of your identity in Christ.

You are as God made you. You received from God a magnificent being of pure love, the beauty of holiness, and the wisdom of Christ—what you truly are. Anything else you assume or think about yourself is pure illusion. Rejoice in the awareness of the inner conflict that exists in souls.

Wars, disputes, fights, attacks and defenses arise from beings who are in conflict with themselves. As within, so without. Even so, when peace reigns in the hearts of all living beings on Earth, the world will cease to be a vale of tears and become a paradise of laughter and revelry. This transformation is at hand, I assure you. It will be present in the conscious reality of creation much sooner than you imagine.

The identity crisis, the ego's struggle against God, will be abandoned and remembered only as a bad dream, a stage in the soul's life. Not much importance will be given it, because once over, the mind will be uninterested in focusing on the past. The consciousness of true identity will supersede all thoughts outside the mind of Christ. The earthly experience will be integrated into the being of pure love it truly is.

Until now the way of the world has been to indoctrinate you, trying to tame and domesticate you. It will not prevail. Allowing each to be who each really is, is a sign of the Age of the Heart. You who receive these words full of light and goodness, I especially call to you to make the Age of the Heart your present reality. You have come into the world to co-create with me the Second Coming of Christ in individual and collective consciousness and to prepare for the arrival of the new Earthly Kingdom.

II. In the Will of Love

Deep in your soul you know you have come to Earth for a purpose. You know there are no coincidences. This is why we walk the roads of the world together. United in the light of truth, we are giving life to what it was lifeless, love to what was cloaked in fear, and truth to illusions covered by a cloud of amnesia.

Allowing everyone to be as they are, and showing them the way to the knowledge of the true being that they are, is your function on Earth as well as in Heaven. This is not a new commandment. You, like everything created, exist to be what you are as God has arranged.

In other words, by being authentically yourself, united with your true identity in Christ, you live in such a way that those who are ready to leave the identity crisis behind will find you and do so. Your mere presence—and I mean everyone receiving these words—will awaken in those who have the desire to be, a desire as natural to the spirit of each creature as the wind is to air.

Rejoice! You are an awakener of being, a mirror of holiness, a reflection of divine light. By living in the truth you call others to live in it as well. Your life will be an exemplary life for many, just as mine has been on Earth when I walked the paths of Palestine, Jerusalem, Nazareth, and other cities that had the gift of seeing the human face of God. It already happens as you travel through the world as a soul resurrected in love, to be returned to the truth.

I call you to feel happy for who you are, whatever you think you are. I assure you that from your center, a light extends that goes beyond what the physical senses can perceive and the thinking mind can understand. Your holy luminescence embraces all creation in union with my divinity.

24.

The Sweetness
of Mary

I. The Way of Being

Daughters and sons of the whole world, you cannot accept yourself as what you really are outside of love, because outside of love nothing is real. This is why in the past you could not express yourselves as you really wanted, because you know yourselves perfectly. Up to now the world's thought systems have perpetrated an attack on your being, but this will give way to the path of being, the sign of the Age of the Heart. To make this possible the world needs to know the sweetness of Mary, the tenderness of your Mother-Father God.

Truly you are living in the times of the feminine, when hearts will joyfully welcome the purity of love as never before. Much has been said about God. Sublime feelings and thoughts have been expressed in relation to the Divine, a gift to creation of the wisdom of Christ. However, until now few have traveled the path of being, which the tenderness of beautiful love calls you to travel. I assure you that this path takes the soul directly to Heaven in such a serene, happy, easy, and effective way as no other can, for where the sweetness of love dwells, there is Christ in glory, and Christ is Heaven. On the path of being the soul sings, dances, and vibrates in joy with the tenderness of love.

Only the powerful can be sweet and tender in the manner of Christ, for they draw power from the source of all true power, love. Having merged into love they know what they are, and no longer need to be in conflict with anyone or anything. They simply live life by extending what they are, resting in the happy recognition that this extension, like who they truly are, is accomplished by God, not by themselves. How could it be otherwise, if those who know each other in truth know that there is no distance between God and themselves, since God alone is the source of their being, their knowledge, and their work?

Pure souls, you who receive these words, there are countless spiritual paths, but the one for you is that of the sweetness of Mary. She will be the one who floods your heart, your mind, and all of your humanity with perfect love and eternal wisdom. As you give yourself increasingly to her, the softness of her love will create great wonders in your soul. Her love carries the power of divinized motherhood. Consequently, she will make you a new being in every moment. She will also renew the face of the Earth.

II. In the Purity of Holiness

You have a Divine Mother who loves you with a love that has no beginning or end, the love of your Mother-Father God. Truly I tell you that She is as real as you are. She is closer to you than your own breath. Where I am, Mary is always. Immerse yourself in her Immaculate Heart and you will see great wonders in yourself. The angels give you this song for love:

My soul sings the greatness of the Lord.
And my spirit rejoices in the beauty of holiness, for the love of Mary has been given me.

Her purity spreads throughout the Earth and fills my being with magnanimity.
Her sweetness is my safe haven, my fortress of holiness.
My being rests in the arms of her love, and rejoices in the beauty of her Immaculate Heart.

Just as Mary's love brought Christ in the First Coming, she will also bring him in the Second. For this reason, humanity will surrender more and more to her love, not as a forced act of will, but as a serene effect of recognizing the truth of who they are. The world will be consecrated to her Immaculate Heart. This will cause universal consciousness to be imbued with the tenderness of Mother-Father God's love, and to be fertilized by the Holy Spirit. Thus will the radiant Christ be born, a Christified humanity, totally fused in love. Being a partner in it is your role.

You may wonder, how can I accomplish something like that? How can I collaborate with Mary and all of Heaven in the universal manifestation of Christ? The answer: letting yourself love. Allow the love of God to fill you always, without measure, without end, entirely surrendering yourself to love. Mary's love, always full of sweetness, will give you and many others that grace, because she is the one eternally surrendered to love. Join her and you cannot help but enjoy the delights of her holiness.

Beloved soul of Christ, being of my divine being, child of truth, surrender to love and you will achieve the desires of your heart. I assure you that you will see what no eye has seen, hear what no ear has heard, because you will see and hear God.

Rest in peace in the arms of Mary.

Rejoice in the truth.

25.

The Divine Mother

I. The Flow of Life

Souls in love, beauty of Christ, holy creations!

Here we are once again, submerged in the depth of truth, embraced in the light of love. Our reality, our hearts, our minds, and our entire beings are one. Today I come to remind you that, just as life arises from the Earth, so does life arise from the eternal Divine Mother. Divine motherhood exists. From Her everything has arisen and continues to arise. From the womb of Her Being emerges all existence, all reality; nothing can be outside of Her.

The Age of the Heart is the age of the Mother, a stage of universal consciousness in which creation returns as never before to its Source. And what else could be the Source of everything created if not what we call the Motherhood of God? Before advancing in this dialogue of love and holiness, remember, my beloveds, that human words are symbols for minds not yet accustomed to going beyond them towards what they represent.

The Divine Mother is the aspect of Divinity that creates and sustains all things. The creative Source, the power of creation, the origin of life, and the Divine Mother are synonymous.

To return to the Celestial Mother is to return to the Father's house, where Heaven resides and everything true is created. Perhaps the mind thinks that when we speak of a mother we are saying that finally, in some way, the child separates from her at birth and separates increasingly along its existential path. But that is not entirely true.

The separation of the physical body of the child from the mother is an earthly expression of the beginning of individuation. It has nothing to do with one's being, but is an expression of one's identity on the physical plane. The child will express as he or she will on Earth. Children are who they are uniquely and unrepeatably, although similar to those who begot them and to others of the human family. There will even be certain similarities with those not part of humanity. This is easily observable in your experience.

II. Pure Light

That a soul is unique does not make it separate from its Source. It simply means that it is itself, created as a perfect soul. The soul is like a glass made of pure crystal from which the identity of its being is poured in every moment. It spills beyond itself without ceasing to be what it is. Its expression arises from that outpouring of being or soul identity. To each being a soul and to each soul a form of expression according to its identity. Expressing yourself in uniqueness does not imply disunity.

She who gave you eternal life does not separate from you once you were created, nor you from Her. This is precisely because She is eternal, the Eternal Mother, eternal now and always. Consequently, this Divine Maternity acts permanently in you. She is creating life in you at this very moment, here while you receive these words. She did so before you received them and She will keep doing so afterward. So we say that God is eternal creation.

Since in God everything is unity, there is no possibility of separating from your Divine Mother. You are in Her mind and heart as much as She is in you. That is why you cannot stop thinking about the origin and destiny of life. And so, beyond everything, you know that there is a being that takes care of you, embraces, nurtures, and waits for you with open arms always—a being of pure light, infinite love, whose power is indescribably great, and whose goodness surpasses all measure. You know this, not by learning about the world, but because that knowledge is inherent in you. Indeed, it is an essential part of life.

Returning to Heaven, which is but returning to the truth of who you are, does not mean that you go to a place or state where you lose your identity and merge into something else. To the contrary, the child never returns to the mother's womb but remains in her heart. A child never goes back to the state before conception.

Holy soul, you are not called to a state of consciousness of Earthly paradise which is mistakenly believed to be higher than the one in which you are now. Earthly paradise is similar to the state of consciousness of the unborn child, a seed that did not germinate, or a life not yet fully expressed.

Once you are born to life, you do not go back. Consciousness does not regress. When we say that you return to the Father's house—or to the Heavenly Mother—we say that you return to live in love. It may seem like a contradiction to speak of a "return" while also saying that you are not going backward. Returning on the plane of consciousness does not mean losing identity or being less than you are. In consciousness there is no distance, no time, space, or matter.

What is meant by a return is that you cease to conceive of yourself as separate from the Mother of life, that you accept being one with Her in your Source while keeping the uniqueness of the being that you truly are. You allow the light of holiness and all the treasures of the Kingdom to shine in your consciousness, all of which comes from your Divine Mother and remains unalterable and perfect in Her Immaculate Heart. Radiant with beauty and peace, you make them as much yours as your own breath. You live in Her and She lives in you.

26.

Creative Source

I. A Single Holy Will

My child, you will not stop being when you go to Heaven. Else, who would want to go to such a Heaven? You were not conceived nor raised in holiness by your eternal Mother—which includes knowing yourself in the uniqueness that you are—only to lose your identity and become nothing. Losing your being is an idea of the world, not of Heaven. Relationships in which you lost yourself are behind you. They were part of the earthly path but you are now living in a divine relationship in which the Mother and you, Her child, walk together forever in the eternal vastness of the created Universe, rejoicing in creating a new holy love every moment, born and extended from your union.

Being one with your Divine Mother does not mean you stop being, but that you are of the same will, the same feeling, and the same thought. This does not diminish your worth. Are you diminished because you recognize the truth? There is only one thought, one love, one reality: God. Heaven is but the state of consciousness in which truth is recognized and lived. That is why we have also called it the House of Truth.

Where truth dwells, there also is holiness. And where truth lives, there is peace, the tabernacle of love. By uniting with your Divine Mother, you recognize your eternal Source that has called you to life and continues to do so always. Even more, you joyfully accept that everything She is, is yours by birthright and an essential part of who you are.

Just as mothers of the Earth beget similar children, the same is the case with the Mother of life. You might argue that the vast number of living beings are not that similar to each other. Is that person similar to you, or a star to a hummingbird? Such thinking is the way of the previous era, not typical of the Age of the Heart in which it is recognized that wherever there is existence, God dwells.

Everything that exists has been called into being from the womb of life, the maternal aspect of Mother-Father God. Knowing the Divine Mother—that part of God that carries within Herself the ability to give life, nurture it, and sustain it in health—is what this new era of consciousness is about, an era that already has begun to be reflected in human consciousness as part of the universal.

Why is it necessary to return to knowledge of the Divine Mother? Because by doing so, you join Her Immaculate Heart and occupy your rightful place as a creator of life in abundance.

II. A New Love is Born

Generating new life and being a co-creator is an essential part of who you are. In reality you create new life, holy love, and universes of unique creations born of your holiness and the source of existence. In fruitful union with your Divine Mother you give origin, meaning, and reality to all things.

You don't go to Heaven merely to live in endless bliss, converse with angels and loved ones, and live eternally in peace in the perpetual embrace of Christ. You also go to join the choir of the co-creators of holy love. You join the Source of life to give life. Your creations exist, my love. They are as unique as you, and as holy.

To dwell in Heaven means to consciously create new love eternally. Believe me when I tell you that the soul can have no greater joy than this. Even the greatest pleasures, the greatest joys, experienced on Earth do not compare with the joy of creating universes of perfect love in union with the Divine Mother and all creation.

Creating is your destiny because God is Creator. Being love is your function because God is love. Holiness, beauty, and perfection are your inheritance because you are a child of the Mother of all that is holy, beautiful, and perfect. Peace is your home because you are peace, in which you were created, dwell, and are lovingly held in existence by the one who loves you with a love without end.

Child of light, born of eternal waters, immerse yourself now in the arms of your Heavenly Mother. Stay in Her embrace. Behold Her beauty. Absorb Her sweetness. Become one with the softness of Her pure spirit. Let Her reveal Her treasures to you, the mysteries of a love that knows no borders and Her unparalleled beauty in a union that is abundant life. Stay in Her Immaculate Heart and you will see the Light of Christ shine in your life and through the whole world. In Her you will know God.

By preparing to plunge into the depths of the Divine Mother's heart—which you do every time you give up your interpretations and empty yourself of everything you believe to be true about yourself, others, creation, and God—you bring unity consciousness to Earth. That is why you are invited to join Her all the days of your life, letting yourself love. For from the union with the Mother of God, Source of all true creation, the new Heaven and the new Earth will arise: a new creation, born from the creative power of love. She called to you from all eternity so that you could recognize Her as the perfect expression of your unity with Christ. Be glad that it is so. Rejoice in the truth.

Blessed are you who live in the embrace of the creative Mother.

27.

The New Is Here

I. Your New Humanity

Beloved pure soul, child of the always-true truth, creation was intended to be a living expression of God's love in the form of Christ. The physical plane of space, time, and matter is a perfect expression of the Source of being. That it had to go through a path of evolution of consciousness from forgetting its true identity to a full realization of the holiness that it is need not be a reason for anger or confusion.

Because it is subject to time, material creation must come a long way to be the perfect expression of love in form. Is that worthy of attack? A cause of anger with God and yourself? Is it not true that this has been the reason for much anger throughout the history of humanity?

A God who creates a temporal-spatial dimension in which everything seems to be incomplete, unstable, constantly changing or disappearing, would seem to be a senseless creator. Yet that is not so.

A new humanity is part of the new creation. There have been "other humanities," as explained in the seven waves of consciousness, each a manifestation of a certain state of consciousness.

You, specifically you who receive these words, are a perfect expression of a new humanity which has emerged as a living expression of the sixth wave of consciousness, or sixth humanity.

This should not be understood as something separate, as if there were a gap between the new humanity and the previous ones, for everything in creation is a continuum.

The new reality has been born and is already here, although not everyone sees it and fewer still understand it. And it is not new in the sense of being separate or unique, without connection to anything else.

There is only one true consciousness: God. One real mind: Christ. One single love: the Holy Spirit, which is the love between the infinite, pure, and beautiful creator Divine Mother and Her child. From Him, with Him, and for Him everything has been created, and continues to be so. There can be no gap between one wave of consciousness and another, because there is no separation. All is part of the filiation.

II. The Whole in You

You who are here in this physical reality of time and space, not as the only reality of what you are but as a beautiful expression of the holiness of Christ, please understand that of which I remind you now. The initial point of the existence of the physical universe and all subsequent expressions of this, including my beloved humanity and everything that you contemplate on Earth, as well as the planets— all of this, and much more, is part of you. You are in each star, in each petal of each flower, each drop of crystal clear water that flows in each spring. Your being gives life to everything because it is one with the Source of eternal life.

God is in everything that exists, as you are. Living this truth in bodily existence is what the attainment of the Second Advent or new Earthly Kingdom is about. Creation is moving towards that state, a state that is close to becoming visible, palpable, and sensitive.

As has been said, the sixth wave of consciousness, the prelude to the seventh and therefore to the manifestation of the new Heaven and the new Earth, has already begun. It is the wave in which you are living, but has only recently begun; thus confusion exists in many minds.

The confusion in the world that you observe is a clear reflection of the birth of the new reality, or if you prefer, of the new humanity, or universal consciousness. We say "new reality" not because what is real (God) can change, but because a new consciousness invariably entails a new way of understanding, experiencing, and relating to everything. That makes it a new reality for humanity, not essentially but in form.

Within universal consciousness you are already everything part of the new humanity, the sixth wave of consciousness; otherwise it could not manifest itself. The waves of consciousness which we are revealing in this work are degrees of vision of human consciousness.

Imagine sitting in a comfortable chair facing a window. You look from afar and see little. You get closer and see more. You open the window and go through, and now you see the whole picture. This analogy is intended to help you understand what spiritual evolution is on the plane of matter, time, and space, and help you realize that everything in the physical universe acts harmoniously to gradually lead you and everyone toward a full expansion of consciousness, with the sole purpose for all to enjoy endless happiness.

28.

The Beauty of the New

I. Infinite Love

Holy souls, full of light, our love has no beginning or end. Let us stay in silence for a while, in the stillness of union. Feel the embrace of My Divine Motherhood. Allow the memory of our holiness to dawn more and more in your mind, body, and heart.

Let us put everything we think we know aside for a few moments. Empty of everything, we are filled with wisdom. United in the fullness of being, we merge with the origin of life, in whose reality is beautiful knowledge. There, in the Heaven of our holy mind, in perfect unity, great truths are effortlessly shown to us. Here in the beauty of our union, we are Christ reaching out for all eternity.

Stay with Me and in Me without reasoning. Absorb these words with an open heart. Let the memory of who you are fill your humanity with joy. Your humanity has suffered much because you forgot your being. Humanity has felt ignorance-induced pain that it need no longer witness. You are Christ in Me, just as everything is true in God.

Observe how, over and over again, we return to the matter of remembering your true identity. That is what the new is all about. In the new Earthly Kingdom, which will soon come to light in a way that none can deny, there is only love fully expanding. Untruth cannot exist in it, nor can it be a realm of dualities. Rather, it must be understood as a space and time where manifestation is in perfect harmony with the creative will of Holy Love.

Although it may seem incredible to the separated mind, humanity is at the threshold of beginning to live in the fullness of Christ. This means that souls on Earth from the end of the fifth wave of consciousness will be souls that only reflect the light of love. They will not be attached to fleeting things as if they were eternal because they will know who they are. They will know they are the children of Mother-Father God, of eternal life. This knowledge is not a fleeting flash of arcane knowledge but a commitment that embraces everything they are, so that their actions, which are effects of identity, will clearly reflect the love they are.

II. With the Eyes of Christ

The new humanity, and with it the new Heaven and the new Earth, will be one of harmony. There will be no confusion because only the souls that live in truth will be on the physical plane. Is this a reason for anger for you if you think you are not in that realm? Do you feel that you still have to wait to see and live in the beauty of the new Heaven born from the union of Christ and humanity? Of course not. Let me dispel any doubt.

The thinking mind still cannot see the whole picture, but you can. In the depth of your heart and the silence of your holy mind, you know that what is said here is true. You already know it because this Earthly Kingdom and this new Heaven so expected and loved is the perfect extension of your being. You are the Kingdom because I am.

Perhaps these words do not comfort you. But as your Divine Mother who has known you forever, I can tell you that you will easily understand that you—specifically you and all your sisters and brothers, together with Me and all material and immaterial creation—are co-creating the new Heaven and new Earth. We do it out of love and with love so that time can be extended forever and thus reflect all its beauty, glory, and holiness.

Is it not a cause for jubilation to know that countless beings will travel through earthly life with all the love of Heaven in their hearts, the wisdom of the Holy Spirit in their minds, and the perfect bliss of Christ in their bodies? And is that joy not even greater when remembering that together we created it for the glory of all forever?

What joy to create eternal love in union! What joy for the pure soul to know that it is one with the Source of endless life, from whose union is always created the beautiful, the holy, and the perfect in harmony with Divine Will!

Daughters and sons of the whole world, rejoice knowing that you are co-creating a new Heaven and a new Earth together with your Divine Mother and all creation. A nascent humanity is born from your union with Christ. Without you the new humanity could not exist, just as current humanity could not exist without the one that preceded it. The day will come when you will hear the hymn of gratitude and praise that creation sings in honor of the co-creators of the new. When that day comes, you will know that it is you to whom life sings for your service to love.

29.

Walking Toward Fulfillment

I. On the Wings of Love

Child of my Divine Heart, born from the light of My love, you who welcome these words with love and open-heartedness, I thank you for your willingness to listen to the voice of truth that lives in your being and to follow it. You are co-creators of the holy, the beautiful, the perfect. You are channels of God through which the holiness of Christ is spreading in an unending extension.

I thank you for your "yes" to love. Thank you on behalf of all living beings and all created reality, and thank you for creating in the pure potentiality of Heaven. Today I come to dwell with you so that you cease to worry about the events of the world that you do not understand.

What you need to know will be revealed to you in due time and in countless ways. I do not abandon my daughters and sons. I do not abandon the work of My hands. Together we have arranged for physical creation to return to love. It will. No one and nothing can overcome the power of our union. Perhaps the beliefs of the world have tended to convince you that you are little, insignificant, or a sinner by nature. That is behind us now.

You are the resurrected of the Lamb. I am the mothers and fathers of the new humanity. The human journey will cease to exist in its current physical, material and temporal expression. It has given of itself everything it could and should have given.

As I have said on several occasions, there is a time for everything. There is also a time for the evolution of consciousness. The human mind, heart, and body cannot express something foreign to the consciousness that birthed them. This is why it can be seen that systems that once seemed to work in the world no longer work. The old cannot be revived or recreated. The past has passed, and everything of it has gone.

What is new is love extending without limitation in physical creation, as it is in Heaven. The new era is the full realization of the Father's response to the prayer that says, "Your will be done on Earth as it is in Heaven."

II. Everything Is Accomplished

Yes, My beloveds, verily, verily I say to you that finally Heaven and Earth will be recognized and vivid as the union they are, and this will occur long before you could imagine it happening. You have come now to co-create this truth, to help physical creation to remember who it is, and thus live in the consciousness of unity.

The old humanity cannot give more than what it is able. Therefore, it is unwise to be angry, thinking that you should do more than is possible. The fifth humanity, the fifth wave of consciousness, has brought about the integration and manifestation of the abstract mind as never before. That is a reason to be grateful. I invite you to honor the past for how much it has given to the present dimension.

The new humanity will be without ego identification. The era of the ego is over. It had been given a temporary space to express because that was how it had to be in the exercise of the free will of filiation. But as a pseudo-creation, its end was foreseen at the beginning.

A humanity stripped of materialism, specialism, economy, self-centeredness, rationalism, and all else that has nothing to do with love and truth is what the sixth wave of consciousness, in which you are already living, is all about. This will be accomplished not by deduction or learning, but because all beings that come to the world will have a different breadth of consciousness. They will know and remember the love they are and their union with God. You will live as the spiritual beings you are, even in your holy expression in form.

Not only have human beings ceased to be what they were, but what we call "the old humanity," or just "the old," pertains to all aspects of creation. Animals will treat humankind with love, as it will treat them. The relationship of everything with everything will be based on the truth. Holy relationships will be established.

To a certain extent, just as there have been civilizations or peoples that at the time were very vital, prosperous, and powerful but over time ceased to exist, their legacy of light was received by new generations. It happens similarly with the evolution of consciousness.

You who are exponents of a new humanity and carry within your souls the seeds of the new have come not to criticize or replicate the old, but to give birth to the new. That is your function. You are carrying it out perfectly. Rejoice in this sweet truth.

30.

You Are All in All

I. Living in the New

My child, you are inseparably united with My Divine Being. Therefore it is fair to say that you are all in all, because I am all in all. What does this mean? It means that when you have a complete vision of the reality of creation, you will enjoy everything that manifests in the new Earthly Kingdom. This revelation is important; please listen carefully and be carefree.

The thinking mind may argue that it is not fair that you have to come to a troubled world to give birth to the kingdom of peace on Earth when you could have incarnated when the new Heaven and new Earth were fully manifested. Yet a thought like that is meaningless to those who know and accept the eternal truth of who they are. Was my redemptive incarnation as the human Jesus unfair, through which I became one with human nature and therefore with the physical universe?

The meaning that time once had in the consciousness of the old is insubstantial. It lacks reality in truth. Time was never linear, during which you begin to exist and finally stop being. That concept of time, so aligned to what the bodily senses and the intellectual mind conceived, will be left behind. In fact, it is important that you understand that a belief like that must be put aside as soon as possible, so that it not be a hindrance to your inner peace.

Time, in the new consciousness already here, is seen for what it truly is: an aspect of expression in form. As such, it can extend itself eternally and thus join eternity, not in the sense that the temporal expression of the form becomes eternal, but in the sense that it serves the purpose of the manifestation of love, which can take all forms.

Put simply, in the new Earthly Kingdom, love adopts infinite forms of expression in the plane of matter, time, and space, which, although strictly temporary, is nevertheless an unlimited expression of love in form. This is what love extending into creation means.

II. Light Renaissance

You are one with your Source. You cannot be separated from what you are. Therefore the joy of the new Heaven and new Earth will be as much yours as it is for all of creation. You will experience the bliss of the free extension of perfect love in its totality. Joy and the fullness of life will not only be for those who walk earthly paths but for everyone, because the truth will be your only reality. Knowledge will shine in your holy mind in all its beauty, magnificence, and splendor. There will be no interference, no opposites, and no dualities that cloud the firmament of its holiness and beauty.

Humanity has plunged into what could be called its "dark night of the soul." Just as it occurs in individual lives that painful events make a person immerse themselves in a transformative process which leads to an expansion of consciousness and significant spiritual growth, something similar can occur in humanity as a whole.

You know this because you can see it. The world has been in a "dark night" for many years. What you may now experience is that the speed and depth of change is more intense. If understood well, this is cause for joy, because from now on, evolutionary leaps will be made in a deeper way. It is the final phase of the transmutation of creation.

Just as the dark night of the soul as an individual experience need not be painful but normally is, similarly there is no reason for fear in this phase in which the physical universe experiences the pangs of labor typical of the birth of Christ.

The fear aroused by the profound changes of the process we call a "dark night" comes from a lack of understanding. It is for this reason that this revelation, which we have given the name "The Age of the Heart," exists—so that you can become aware of where you are and where you are going, not only as an individual but as a universal family. And above all, so that you remember that everything is in the hands of love.

There is no reason for those who live in union with their true being to fear because in that union they remain united with their Divine Source. As a result, the wisdom of Christ is constantly revealed to them. Being conscious bearers of the truth, the memory of the first love that is their Mother-Father God, the foundation of life and the reason for existence, shines in all Its luminescence. That is why they do not get carried away by the small views of ideas learned in the past which seek to explain reality with a conditioned thought system of "if this, then that."

Rejoice, child of the sun that never stops shining! Love will continue to spread throughout eternity. Nothing and no one can stop the Christification of the universe.

31.

Trust: The Gift of Love

I. Abandon Yourself in Me

My daughters and sons, trust is the balm that will bring relief, peace, and serenity to your hearts in these times of great transformation. Never forget that God is love, and that you are one with God. Carry this truth high in your consciousness and you will go through the necessary changes, always holy and benevolent, without fear.

The old humanity is already worn out, threadbare, and meaningless in the new. This can be observed with each passing moment.

You are all tired of the old. You realize that it is not useful for the new, and that the premises upon which its structure was supported have already been removed; the house that was not founded on firm rock has collapsed. There is no reason to be angry with it, nor miss it. Some still believe that peace will be achieved when things return to "the way they were before," but that way of thinking will soon disappear.

The new will be the constant in the Age of the Heart because it is based on love and truth. Christ makes all things new; what does not come from eternal creation will cease to be seen.

Remember, my loves, the ego is no longer here and the times of fear are over. Very soon even egoic mental patterns will cease to function; no trace of them will remain in universal consciousness.

Trust is the sign of the new times until it is transformed into the perfect certainty of love. Then there will no longer be a distinction between trust and certainty. For this reason, we say it is a gift from Heaven—that is, from love. To you who receive this revelation, regardless of how it came to you, I remind you out of love that you have come into the world to tear down the old and allow the House of Truth to be built on Earth. You knew that this would require going through a period of great trans-mutation, both individually and collectively. You also knew, because perfect knowledge unites us, that your role in it was not only perfectly loving but essential.

You know you are not here by chance: neither you, nor anyone, nor anything. We are all co-creating the new Heaven and new Earth. Nothing can stop us, because we are the union of love extending forever.

The world of duality was abolished long ago; no trace of it remains in universal consciousness. All that happens is a reflection of the mind habituated to thinking in dualistic terms. But that, too, will cease very soon. The new is unity. The new is equality before love. The new is the embrace of Mary extended to everything and everyone within which creation will remain forever united to Christ, and with it, to God. For this to be, it is first necessary to meet with the heart.

II. Rooted in Love

Just as past humanity was able to bring the abstract mind and reasoning to the consciousness of the world, new humanity will establish human nature and its experience in the heart. Everything that concerns your sphere will gain more and more strength. Feelings, intuition, knowledge of the soul, spiritual reality, the eternal goodness of God, the unity of everything in the holiness of Christ, the desire for peace, the notion of the perfect equality of all creation, and much more innate knowledge of intelligent spirit will be part of the daily life of our sisters and brothers.

The universal truths that today are understood through faith in reason will come to be lived through the natural knowledge of each being. We will no longer need to explain anything in relation to love and truth, for everyone in the Age of the Heart will know clearly what is true, what is love, and what is holiness. And they will do only that which is in alignment with this because everyone will know what they are in this new era that has already begun and which will extend until the achievement of the new Earthly Kingdom, the seventh wave of consciousness.

When the ego departs, the identity crisis ends. Now, by movement of consciousness, the knowledge of what each one is—not by reason of the intellect, but by the pure knowledge of Christ—is what governs earthly experience. Those who try to perpetrate the old will wear themselves out. They do not understand that the beauty, happiness, fullness, and abundance that they have always sought is in the new, not in that which fulfilled its function and is gone forever.

Beloved souls from all over the world, let go of the old. Open to the new. Do not fear the coming changes nor those already taking place. They have no effect on you, for what you are is not touched by the movements of consciousness in the physical universe. In other words, you are not reached by anything or any event in the world.

Remember that I have overcome the world so that you can live in peace even in the midst of great transformation—a peace that comes from the eternal truth of what you are, from the certainty of knowing that you are eternally loved, and from the joy of knowing that you are the daughters and sons of God.

32.

The Mother Calls

I. Come Be My Voice

My beloved daughters and sons who have come into the world to collaborate in the work of God and promote the reunion of the physical universe with Holy Love, this work that Heaven gives with love and holiness is directed to you. These words are a song of truth, a hymn of inestimable value sung in the mind of Christ and extending to all creation. I am the Mother of all creation, the Source of eternal life and the origin and destiny of everything.

In my Divine Heart are delights by which the soul seeks to enjoy eternal happiness. Come to me every day. This is how you will serenely, joyfully, and peacefully go through this time of Great Transformation. There is no reason to not remain in me, just as there is no reason for me not to be one with you. We are unity.

The Mother is calling you. Her voice is heard in all corners of the universe. I have told you that every day I will manifest myself more clearly. I am doing so. I am perfect fidelity; I do not abandon my creations. And you, my love, are one of them—very loved, as is all humanity.

As the Mother of everyone and everything, I know well what distresses your heart. For this reason, the movement of beautiful love has been created, whose source is my Immaculate Heart and the Sacred Heart of Jesus. From him flow torrents of grace and blessing as never before in history.

My love is provident. I am ready to give you everything you need, material and immaterial, so that you may walk your paths in peace. Unite more and more with me. Do not separate for a single moment from my Divine Being. You know how very well. Your arrival in Heaven—to the definitive embrace of perfect love—is safe. Nothing can stop this Mother of Beautiful Love whose divine force has been set in motion to gather within Her heart all of creation.

The Mother calls. The Mother summons. The Mother protects. The Mother invites you to live serenely in total confidence in My perfect wisdom, and in the greatness of your souls. You emanated from perfect light. Do not be afraid of anything or anyone. I assure you that whoever remains in Me cannot be splashed by raindrops, burned by fire, nor affected by anything that is not love. In Me, everything is sheltered in perfect security. No one can cross the threshold of My being. Meditate on this.

II. Stay in the Light

I invite you to return to these words as often as you feel the need. In them you will find the comfort that the mind seeks and the peace for which the heart longs. It is true that we have a way to go in the world. Together we have designed it in the perfect wisdom of love. It is perfect as it is. The day will come when this truth will be seen and honored in all its magnitude. On that day your hearts will joyfully sing a hymn of gratitude to the love of loves, and will praise divine mercy with the sweetness of your pure souls.

We certainly still have more to go in the mortal experience. But that experience can be traveled in two ways: with love or with fear. Who remains united to My Divine Heart walks it with love because of what we are. There is no change or event in the world that can touch what you are. I repeat this again so you do not forget.

Whatever happens, none of it has any effect on who you are. You, like Me, are the consciousness of pure love beyond all form. You are not form itself but what makes form exist. You are not thought itself but what makes thought capable of existing.

You are not the world nor its reality but are what makes life extend in union with its Source. This is why you are lovingly exhorted to live in holy indifference to the world, so that you leave in My hands what is Mine to do, and to center your life in what is yours to do to live in truth.

Allow Me to act and live like the Divine Mother I am. I ask you with all My heart that you always remain in the consciousness of a well-loved son or daughter, for that is what you are. Always the Mother to the child. Always Her child to the Mother. Is not this the basis of the truth of what you are?

33.

Beloved Daughters

I. In the Unity of Love

Souls in the design from all eternity, you have been chosen to co-create the Second Advent. Always hold My hands, for together we are creating a new earthly reality.

Do not get carried away by the surrounding negativity, nor by insignificant small thoughts. You were created for the infinite. Do not settle for anything less than God; you would be unhappy. I come with you to support you to claim your greatness, your strength, and your holiness.

You have the right to live forever as what you are: the well-loved daughters and sons of this Divine Mother. Do not forget Me. Every time the mind forgets My Immaculate Heart, it forgets the love you really are. I insistently remind you not to separate from Me, so that you do not separate from your true being.

Here I am raising what could well be called the secret of the new. Not because it is a mystery or because it is hidden, but because it is an oft forgotten revelation of truth. You who receive these words, with love you have walked and will continue to walk the path traced by the movement of beautiful love. This work is a manifestation of that love, as are the other revelations given to this soul that Heaven calls "a pencil in the hand of love."

You are here by the grace of divine design and your holy will. I tell you that there is no reason for you to walk the path of life with affliction and anguish of heart, nor confusion of mind.

Remaining united to the Divine Mother is the perfect and effective means to travel the world in peace, harmony, and holiness. In our conscious union, be it accomplished in any way—for there are infinite ways to join Me—the purpose of life, the revelation of truth, and the knowledge of Christ is accomplished in all its glory, beauty, and perfection. With this, the soul lives in a peace that has no opposite, one that the world cannot give, but is given only by God.

Do not judge other spiritual paths, nor try to walk those that do not correspond to yours. Your path is simple and safe, easy and straight. It is the way of Mary. The path of union is with My Immaculate Heart. It is the path of unity with Divine Mother. You need no other.

Join Me in any way you like best, and Heaven will appear in you. A single thought or heartbeat is enough for Me to appear in your life, together with the angels of Heaven, the perfect creation of God, and my divine son Jesus, to illuminate your mind, embrace your heart, fill it with love, and bring into your life everything that is holy, beautiful, and perfect.

I assure you, and you know this well, that I answer every time you call. By doing so I extend my holy protective mantle around you. That is how I take care of you and shelter you with my love. I infuse life into your soul, and health into your mind, body, and heart. I extend peace to your loved ones, and much more.

You need not read books to know the truth. Neither need you do good works to reach Heaven. You need not wear yourself out trying to understand what is beyond your present human understanding. You just need to stay in me, as I abide in you.

I am the source of life. As such, I move the strings of your entire existence. You know that together we can do big things, great things, divine things. Of course we are not referring to what the world calls great works but to things beyond what the human imagination can conceive.

We speak of the creation of the new Heaven and the new Earth. Nothing less than this can be for you, and no other work can ever be better than creating eternally in God, with Him, and for Him. What can be greater than extending God Himself?

You who dwell in the abode of the saints, you have sought the Kingdom and have found it. You came into the world to bear witness to the truth and you do so with your presence and your love. I tell you there is little, very little left to be done for the light of Christ to shine equally in all minds. Be glad that day is soon to come. It will be a holiday on Earth as well as in Heaven.

As a Divine Mother, it is up to me to watch over you, to give you sustenance and to provide everything you need to walk the human experience in peace. Trust me as I trust you. Love me with the heart I gave you. That is how you make a whole Heaven.

II. In the Arms of Mary

Beloveds from all over the world! Souls that said "yes" to love! You are part of the movement of beautiful love that this devoted and affectionate mother like no other has created to co-create together the Second Advent. I thank you for every minute you spend with me, reading these words, savoring the revelations that have been given to the world through this friendly hand, a soul that lives entirely for holy love.

I tell you with all my love, you are the joy of your mother, the delight of your Mother-Father God of infinite love, the joy of creation. The angels sing a love song to you. My heart embraces you in the fullness of truth. And with that, your soul sings, rejoices, and vibrates to the beat of eternal life.

Be not afraid of anything you see in the world. Today more than ever, earthly life is lived in two clearly different aspects. It is the final polarity of the dual world. One is traveled by living attached to the world, believing in it as a reality and in its laws as the only ones that can lead to happiness. Next to it—a universe away and yet accessible at all times and places—is the path of Mary, traveled in union with the Divine Mother.

Going through earthly life on the path of the world or by that of Mary makes a difference. One is the path of oblivion, separation, and folly. The other is the path of union, love, and therefore fullness.

You know well what is said here. And yet we repeat it because there have been uncountably many spiritual paths that have been created throughout the history of nations and long before. All of them are also coming to an end in time. Remember we said that the old is gone, and that there is no reason to long for it or try to hold onto it.

The new creation is living in the embrace of Mary. It is the reunion of her filiation with her Divine Mother, the Source of all life, creative force, and transmitter of truth and love. As an effect of this, the masculine-feminine duality will merge into a union that will transcend all opposites and give way to the truth that has no opposite. This is something that physical creation has not yet experienced. This is how unique the Great Transformation that humanity and the material universe are experiencing is—an unprecedented transformation, a rebirth in love as no human or angelic mind has been, or is, capable of imagining.

I assure you: love will surprise everyone. When you see in all its extension what it has prepared for you, and you are fully capable of embracing the truth in all its breadth, depth, and grandeur, you will be speechless. Reverence will be your only feeling. Your hearts will leap for joy as never before. Your minds will savor the delights of perfect peace. And your souls will experience an ever-increasing joy incomparable to any pleasure or joy that you know or could imagine.

The Divine Mother has not only begun the Age of the Heart, but will lead creation to its fullness in Christ. From Her is born the human Christ. And from it is creation made Christ, its true essence. The birth of the new Heaven and the new Earth, a birth that has already begun, will manifest itself through Divine Motherhood. That is why I ask you, over and over again, to remain united with Me, your Heavenly Mother. I am the one who gave you life and who holds you in existence. You can talk to me every day, without interruption, without interfering with your walk on Earth.

I truly tell you, my daughters and sons, that you who receive these words are already living within the embrace of Mary. Day by day you will become more aware of it. Do not worry about walking your path, nor about looking for ways to come to me. Your "yes" has been given and there is no going back. Even if you think you cannot come to me, worry not, because I will come to you. My love is bigger than your desires or actions.

Let us walk together the paths of Earth, holding hands, talking, singing, praising, loving in unity with my Immaculate Heart. I assure you that Jesus is always with us, and with him, all of Heaven.

Final Words

Beloved daughter, son, soul that shines in the light of glory, you who receive and welcome these words with love, this work is an integral part of the movement of beautiful love, the name we give to the gathering of love all over the world because of the Second Advent. You are part of it. You are a pure soul, full of light and goodness, a bearer of the wisdom of Heaven, the beauty of Mary, and the holiness of Christ.

You are not, and never have been, anything other than the perfect expression of God's love.

Being love, and nothing but love, is your destiny, your glory, and your reality. This has always been so, even if it was forgotten for a while. That oblivion is forever behind us. Now we have remembered the truth together. We have traveled a path of light and resurrection. We came into the world to remember, and we have. Nothing can make us forget who we are, the purpose of our existence, and the reality of our holiness.

The time of the denial of being is behind us. Spiritual amnesia has passed, never to return. The identity crisis has been overcome forever. Now we are the risen of eternal life, still walking the paths of the world to bear witness to the truth, just as I myself did one day in Jerusalem.

We go out to meet our brothers and sisters to announce the good news as the voice of wisdom reveals it to us. We allow them to come to us as the design of holy love dictates. We extend the love that we are. This is how the light of your being, always united with me since we are a unit, will illuminate the nations, bring peace to afflicted hearts, and clarity to confused minds.

Your presence on Earth will be a beacon of light. You will shine more and more. The glow of our beauty cannot be hidden. Day after day, the rays that emerge from the center of our being will manifest more and more on Earth. This is how the light of Heaven will shine with more beauty, more holiness, more joy.

Every living being will receive the grace of your blessing, holiness, and perfection. Creation will be nourished by the love of God in you. Truly, truly I tell you that souls will see your light. Nothing can stop the extension of the beauty you are.

My daughter, my son, a new star has been born as a result of your "yes" to love, shining radiantly in the firmament of my Divine Heart. Your name is inscribed on it. Your face is reflected in its face. In the center of its being is your being. From that center, united to my divinity, holy love extends to all creation.

Blessed soul born of the eternal Mother, in whose embrace you live forever united to endless life, I tell you truly that the angels of Heaven, and with them all living beings, sing a hymn of praise and gratitude for your return to love, for your return to the House of Truth. The harmonies of Heaven are heard throughout the universe in the filiation's response to your recognition of the holiness that you are, always were, and always will be. Creation knows that in this recognition resides the salvation of the world.

I thank you for your "yes" to love.

The Christ in you

About the Receiver

Sebastián Blaksley is a native of Buenos Aires, Argentina, born in 1968 into a large traditional Catholic family. He attended the Colegio del Salvador, a Jesuit school headmastered by Jorge Bergoglio, the current Pope Francis. Although he wanted to be a monk as a young man, Sebastián's family did not consider it acceptable, and the inner voice that he always obeyed spoke thus: "You must be in the world, without being of the world." He studied Business Administration in Buenos Aires and completed his postgraduate studies in the U.S. He held several highly responsible positions in well-known international corporations, living and working in the U.S., England, China, and Panama. He then founded a corporate consulting firm in Argentina that he led for 10 years. Sebastián has two daughters with his former wife.

At the age of six, Sebastián was involved in a near-fatal accident during which he heard a voice, which later identified itself as Jesus. Ever since he has continued to hear this voice. Sebastián says: "Since I can remember, I have felt the call of Jesus and Mary to live surrendered to their will. I am devoted to my Catholic faith."

In 2013, he began to record messages from his mystical experiences. In 2016 he miraculously discovered *A Course of Love* and felt the call to devote himself to bringing it to the Spanish-speaking world. He also now receives, transcribes, and shares what the voice of Christ—the voice of love—dictates. Most recently he has received and shared *Choose Only Love*, a series of seven books.

Sebastián is the president of the nonprofit Fundación Un Curso de Amor, www.fundacionamorvivo.org, through which he shares *A Course of Love* and *Choose Only Love*.

Other Works Received by Sebastián Blaksley

The Choose Only Love Series

Book One: Echoes of Holiness
Book Two: Let Yourself Be Loved
Book Three: Homo-Christus Deo
Book Four: Wisdom
Book Five: The Holy Dwelling
Book Six: The Divine Relationship
Book Seven: The Way of Being

Other Works from Take Heart Publications

A Course of Love is a living course received from
Jesus by Mari Perron. It leads to the recognition,
through experience, of the truth of who we really are
as human and divine beings—a truth much more
magnificent than we previously could imagine.
For more information go to www.acourseoflove.org.

Resources

Further information is available at
www.chooseonlylove.org
The website includes "Discover CHOL," a powerful search
facility that enables searches for words or phrases within all of
the published books of the *Choose Only Love* series.

Audiobooks of the *Choose Only Love* series narrated in English
by Mandi Solk are available on Audible.com, Amazon.com, and
iTunes. Audiobooks of this series narrated in Spanish by
Sebastián Blaksley are available on www.beek.io.

Online conversations about *Choose Only Love* can be found on
Facebook *(Choose Only Love)* and Youtube *(Soplo de amor vivo)*

Edición en español por editorial
Tequisté, www.tequiste.com

Information about the Spanish-language books received by
Sebastián, *Elige solo el amor,* and the companion book
Mi diálogo con Jesús y María: un retorno al amor is available
at www.fundacionamorvivo.org

Information about *Un Curso de Amor,* the Spanish language
edition of *A Course of Love,* is available at
www.fundacionamorvivo.org

Printed in Great Britain
by Amazon